How to Make Your
Analyst Love You

How to Make Your Analyst Love You

A Guide to Becoming a More Appealing Neurotic

DR. THEODOR SARETSKY

A Citadel Press Book
Published by Carol Publishing Group

A Citadel Press Book
Published by Carol Publishing Group
Citadel Press is a registered trademark of Carol Communications, Inc.
Editorial Offices: 600 Madison Avenue, New York, N.Y. 10022
Sales & Distribution Offices: 120 Enterprise Avenue, Secaucus, N.J. 07094
In Canada: Canadian Manda Group, P.O. Box 920, Station U, Toronto, Ontario M8Z 5P9
Queries regarding rights and permissions should be addressed to Carol Publishing Group, 600 Madison Avenue, New York, N.Y. 10022

Carol Publishing Group books are available at special discounts for bulk purchases, for sales promotions, fund raising, or educational purposes. Special editions can be created to specifications. For details contact: Special Sales Department, Carol Publishing Group, 120 Enterprise Avenue, Secaucus, N.J. 07094

Manufactured in the United States of America
10   9   8   7   6   5   4   3   2   1

Library of Congress Cataloging-in-Publication Data

Saretsky, Theodor, 1932–
    How to make your analyst love you : a guide to becoming a more appealing neurotic / by Theodor Saretsky.
        p.   cm.
    "A Citadel Press Book."
    ISBN 0–8065–1412–4
    I. Title.
PN6231.P78S27   1993
818'.5402—dc20   92–38086
                                                        CIP

As a rule, when I am attacked I can defend myself,
but when I am praised I am absolutely helpless.
—SIGMUND FREUD, 1911

What I have wanted throughout my life is to come
closer to people in a human way rather than be
admired like a rock against which the waves break
in vain.
—SIGMUND FREUD, 1928

Contents

Acknowledgments

To begin with, I want to extend my special thanks to my wife, Dr. Lorelle Saretsky, for her patience, interest, and constructive suggestions while I was absorbed for so long on this project. Corinne Boni, my faithful typist, waded through enough drafts so that by now she has the equivalent of a summa cum laude neurosis. Sybil Carlin helped me to edit and organize the book, and her sense of humor succeeded in mellowing out some of my weightier material. Dr. Robert Mendelsohn, my son-in-law, provided wild flights of imagination that took me to places that would never have occurred to me in my own waking life. Eileen Diamond's sensitive artwork provided a nice light touch to the book, and Rich Kopstein's photography was much appreciated.

Thanks are also due to Drs. Katz, Epstein, Feiner, Herman, Gilman, Stockhammer, Sussal, and Linda Robbins, all of whom vainly tried to restore me to sanity. Finally, Gail Kinn and Kevin McDonough, both fine editors, are to be complimented for making up the final score: Ego 4, Id 2.

Foreword

This book advises the hard-core certified masochist, the guaranteed loser in life, how to turn his or her various symptoms and complaints into an advantage. The author, renowned psychoanalyst Dr. Theodor Saretsky, takes you behind the couch and candidly reveals how to develop a more friendly unconscious, entertaining, upscale symptoms, and an appealing neurosis that analysts can really learn to appreciate.

It doesn't matter whether you are an oral-sadist who has lost his bite, a classical psychonudnick, or an altogether draining, impossible person. All that is required to receive more than the "normal cure" is to provide your analyst with a "good hour" by making him feel better than he did when you first came in.

Following the tactics and strategies described in this book and developed by Dr. Saretsky during more than forty years of clinical experience, you will learn how to get interpretations that favor you over your wife, how to have the most fascinating dreams imaginable, and how to finally be on life's A list.

Haven't you ever wondered about those fortunate few who become memorable patients—those who rarely get their fees raised, who see their analysts during prime time, and who always seem to get a warm welcome even from the analyst's answering machine?

This book guarantees even the most infantile, self-absorbed patient that he is capable of rising above common self-pity and of getting his analyst to love him. Every analyst needs someone to understand him, and that person could be you.

Dr. Saretsky offers a rare glimpse into the analyst's tortured psyche and suggests that analysts are only human beings in disguise. If you treat yours with the tact and sensitivity that his fragile ego requires, it won't be long before he asks you to fill in his Sunday tennis game.

Among the topics covered are: Secrets to Making a Good First Impression on the Phone, Guerrilla Warfare in the Waiting Room, What to Do If You Remind the Analyst of His First Wife, The Analyst's Family, Having the Right Dreams, The Most Popular Childhood Traumas, How to Have Interesting Insights, Should You Refer Your Best Friend?, Sex in the Analytic Hour, Analyst Types to Beware Of, How to Terminate Without Hurting Your Analyst's Feelings.

Already, seventeen readers of this book have been permanently enshrined in the Patient Hall of Fame, thirty miles south of Vienna. Wouldn't you like to join them?

In real life Dr. Saretsky is a practicing psychoanalyst, a clinical professor in Adelphi University's Postdoctoral Institute, and a diplomate in clinical psychology. He has written three books, including *Sex as a Sublimation for Tennis — From the Secret Works of Sigmund Freud* (Workman Publishing), and many chapters and journal articles on various psychoanalytic topics.

                                                        F. A. BLUNGETT, M.D.

From Me to You

I have a little symptom
It does not go away,
I have a little symptom,
And I will make you pay.
It bothers me on trains
On public buses too,
As long as it keeps bothering me
I'll keep on bothering you.
I'll annoy you in the morning
I'll annoy you every day.
I'll annoy you till my symptoms
Have up and gone away.
And after all is said and done
And all annoying through,
I wouldn't be at all surprised
That you'll have symptoms too.

In *Even Further Studies in Hysteria* (1905)
by Sigmund Freud
—A poem received from Emma von R.,
his only treatment failure

Note to Readers

Freud is the father of psychoanalysis.
It had no mother.

GERMAINE GREER

Some readers may interpret the use of the masculine pronoun "he" to refer to analysts in this book as a reflection of the misogynist attitude of many psychoanalysts and of the overwhelming male-chauvinist bias of the profession.

The Board of Directors of SICR wishes to deny those assertions, even though they are true.

How to Make Your
Analyst Love You

CHAPTER I

Are You Worth Analyzing? Or, Who Is SICR?

Sanity is madness put to good use.

G. SANTAYANA

Do you have an absolutely insufferable personality? Is it your misfortune to be fixated at what Sigmund Freud once referred to as the "psychonudnick" stage of development? When analysts gather during August to confide in one another about their trials and tribulations, does your name invariably crop up?

In his classic study of the unconscious, *Thirty Years Beneath the Couch* (1934), Freud noted that "some neuroses are just not fair." To this very day, many neurotics are so self-absorbed and inconsiderate that they fail to realize that their analyst is only human.

Perhaps unwittingly, you fall into the category of what has been euphemistically called "the difficult patient." Are you an incurable grievance collector, a dedicated masochist, or a passive-aggressive manipulator? Or do you have an even more insidious problem: a dull neurosis with few redeeming features? Perhaps your oral sadism has lost its bite. Maybe you've forgotten the punch line to the tale of heartbreaking events that lead up to your favorite early childhood trauma, the "cold enema" story. To put it as kindly as possible, maybe your analyst is sorry he ever started working with you.

Check for telltale signs. Does your analyst frequently call you by the wrong name? Has he forgotten your appointment

1

for three consecutive sessions? Have you driven him back into analysis? Has your fee been raised every month or your time been cut back to fifteen minutes?

Has even his answering machine begun to sound rejecting?

You may not be paranoid; your analyst actually may not like you.

Don't be naive enough to think that successful analysis consists of simply taking your chances and hiring someone objective to solve all your problems. What if you remind the analyst of his ex-wife?

While it is true that analysts are generally warm, caring individuals, they are not immune to the normal range of emotions. It should come as no surprise that they see you as all the other people you've aggravated over the years see you. The fact that they're more scientific simply means they'll dislike you for far better reasons.

Think of your poor parents, who slaved and sacrificed for you, and all the thanks they got. It wasn't just that you felt guilty toward them, you *were* guilty.* Why else would the relatives have unanimously voted you out of the cousins' club? And would anybody else in the world think it's a compliment when his wife tells him that he gave her an anticlimax?

Is there any hope then for the *schmegegge*, the *kvetch*, or the chronic pestimist?† Not if you continue to think of yourself as a victim. Sigmund Freud was fond of quoting an old Icelandic proverb, "Every man likes the smell of his own farts." There's no particular virtue in blindly repeating your faults. In fact, it's rather malicious. Until very recently, your prospects would have been dim indeed. New promising psychoanalytic discoveries suggest, however, that it is possible for even the most trying neurotics to have a reasonable chance of success of getting their analysts to love them. You, too, can finally be-

---

*An overwhelming body of clinical research conclusively proves that mental illness is genetic; parents inherit it from their children.

†Psychoanalytic terminology for patients who have a special talent for getting on the analyst's nerves and under his skin.

come an unforgettable experience, even a personal favorite. One day your analyst might eagerly look forward to seeing you, might offer you his unlisted number, may miss you terribly during August, and never again consider raising your fee.

The Indomitable Neurotic—SICR

Imagine yourself on a couch with a good view, becoming a chapter in your analyst's next book, always getting interpretations that give you the benefit of the doubt, and being one of those wonderfully neurotic people whose analyst completely forgets himself and says, "You're really a piece of work, I think you're terrific!"

How is this monumental task to be accomplished? Simply by applying the principles developed by the Saretsky Institute for Counselor Rehabilitation—SICR.

SICR was originally founded in 1982 to prevent "analytic burnout" by training more highly motivated patients to learn how to be kinder and more considerate toward their analysts. The types of neuroses presented by modern patients were proving so stressful to analysts that many were developing more severe symptoms than their patients. An obsessive analyst that I know is still undecided between MCI, Sprint, and AT&T long distance, so he subscribed to all three. Another analyst who had tipped over the edge found himself saying to a new patient, "Well, let's drop the cat down the well and see how long it takes her to splash." One cannot easily measure the emotional toll of working with an entire caseload of people like yourself.

Obviously, some neurotics lack common sense. If they would drop their self-pity and forget the bitterness of failed sibling rivalries and parental rejection, their personalities might be far more appealing. The Saretsky Institute for Counselor Rehabilitation was founded expressly to make the relationship between patient and analyst more compatible, to help you, the perennial failure, make your personality work best for you.

We believe that any patient can learn to be more fun—not

just the jet-set celebrities and beautiful people with glamorous lives, or the dramatic storytellers whose life experiences unfold like a Russian novel, or the sexy patients with lurid fantasies about simultaneous orgasms, or even the yuppies with extra tickets for football games and hot stock tips.

SICR is also dedicated to relieving the misplaced guilt and TMJ suffered by dedicated professionals who are tormented by the foolish thought that they may have done something wrong when they wanted to leap across the couch and strangle a whining patient with their bare hands.

The obvious response to such self-recrimination is "Nonsense!" Like a mother who favors one of her children over the others, an analyst cannot help but like the patients who really deserve it.

Psychosemitic Disorders— The Bane of the Analyst's Existence (with apologies to Leo Rosten)*

What is wrong with most people? Oddly enough, the most common maladies cannot be found in formal textbooks or

---

*Leo Rosten, *The Joys of Yiddish* (New York: Random House, 1967).

within the pages of the *Diagnostic & Statistical Manual* to be found on the desk of every psychoanalyst. A psychoanalyst can usually tell what's wrong with you as soon as you walk in the door. It's the same thing your wife's been telling you for the last twenty years: You're a schmuck, or maybe a schlemiel.

The analyst will never give you this diagnosis to your face. Why? Are you going to pay someone $125 an hour to call you a schmuck when your wife will do it for free? The medical doctor calls it an upper respiratory infection, not a cold. He knows patients want a fancy name for what ails them so he can charge them a proper fee for treating it.

What follows is a secret list, circulated only among professionals until now, of the most common aggravating neurotic disorders. Freud fondly referred to this group as *farshlepte kranks*—people with long, drawn out, intractable disorders. In the professional literature, you will only find the much milder term "negative therapeutic reactions." This refers to patients whose symptoms become more severe when the analyst expresses hope for their eventual cure or praises their progress. Paradoxically, the better the patients seem to be, the worse they get.

Kvetch. This type of neurotic will wear the analyst down by attrition. Possessed of an incomparable assortment of "grepses," groans, shrugs, and moans, these patients can make the simple act of agreeing on an appointment time or setting a fee an excruciating experience. Everything is difficult or impossible; no suggestion has the desired effect.

Mishegass. The kind of madness signified by mishegass is mostly in a lighter vein—utter nonsense, an absurd belief, even a crazy conviction; usually regarded by the analyst in a sort of indulgent way.

"Your penis is shrinking? Okay, your penis is shrinking. Everybody's penis is shrinking. The world is shrinking!"

Over a five-year period, an inhibited young woman was torturing herself by obsessing about the rights and wrongs of sleeping over at her boyfriend's (now her fiancé's) house. "Why not?" asked the analyst. The girl blushed. "Well, I just know I'll hate myself in the morning." The analyst, who had gently indulged her guilty indecisiveness all along, finally got impatient and said, "So sleep late!"

Nebbish. A sad sack, a loser. When the nebbish leaves the room, the analyst feels a fascinating patient just came in.

Psychonudnick. Someone who bores, pesters, nags, and annoys, all at the same time. Tolerable, though. Unlike the Repeater, the psychonudnick gets under your skin but doesn't eat your heart out.

Schlemiel. Hard-luck type; a submissive and uncomplaining victim; congenitally maladjusted. A born loser. Frequently arrives late for the session complaining that he has so many problems, he doesn't know where to start. Then, at the end of the hour, he asks if the analyst wouldn't mind staying a little late.

Schnook. A passive, unassertive type; ineffectual but deadly.

Schmegegge. Combines the worse qualities of the schlemiel and the psychonudnick. Passive in a hyperkinetic way. An untalented neurotic. Disturbs everyone else's session with his loud, jovial voice in the waiting room.

Schnorrer. A compulsive bargainer, a chiseler. Has a remarkable talent for exploiting and assuaging one of the most powerful forces in the psyche of the analyst: guilt. The check is always "in the mail." Takes a first class trip around the world but still manages to get the analyst to see him at a reduced fee.

Since Freud's time, of course, other neurotic types have been discovered.

The Metaphiliac. These individuals engage in a pervasive search for more meaning than exists. They are recognized as the "Typhoid Marys" of stress. They carry it but are unaffected by it after they pass it on to you. They are happy and mellow only when they are creating a problem.

The Inverted Paranoid. They feel that they are not good enough to be followed or persecuted by anyone.

Pretraumatic Stress Syndrome. These individuals are

anxious because of the knowledge that since nothing bad is happening to them, something is sure to happen soon.

The Reverse Paranoid. They suffer from the belief that they are following or persecuting somebody.

Vegetarian Personality. This group consists entirely of male anorexics. These individuals are utterly confused. There is no literature on them, no one has ever heard of them, no one even thinks they exist. The loneliness, the despair, the disorientation that comes from an illness that shouldn't be, is impossible to describe in words alone. The aversion to eating the meat of dead animals is a particular problem to the adult who, as a child, hated to eat his vegetables.

The One Constant in a Changing World

For those patients who are willing to overhaul their marketing strategy, SICR offers sound advice and instruction on how to cultivate a bold and original neurosis. Wouldn't you like to learn how to be eminently quotable, to make absolutely great Freudian slips? Would you be interested in developing an incomparable imagination that elevates your neurosis to such heroic proportions that you could knock your analyst down with a fender (whoops) feather?

Based on years of intensive interviews and careful research with recovered analysts, we have constructed a scientific profile of the kind of patient who would be practically irresistible, a pleasant interlude, and a welcome addition to any analyst's practice. In 1989, the American Psychiatric Association even named a new neurosis after one of our outstanding graduates. Highlight films of his course of treatment were recently shown on *Donohue* and *Inside Edition*.

All that is needed is hard work and the faithful application of the precepts outlined here. But it will not be easy. As Alfred Adler so delicately put it, "If you want chicken soup, first you have to kill a chicken." To understand the essence of being an analyst is to grapple with what it takes to be a saint and a wise man while working from a small, cramped office that is not rent-controlled, has an air conditioner that frequently breaks down, and depends on a landlord who has never been in analysis.

Freud's biographer, Peter Gay has called psychoanalysts the "detectives of absences; the absolute guardians of subjects dropped, overtures rejected, silences prolonged." As I hope to demonstrate, you don't really have to be hip, hot, and happening to clean up your act and avoid the hot water that one patient got himself into when he told his analyst, "I really *depreciate* you." You just have to possess a little common sense and a good-natured neurosis. our motto is "Even a paranoid can learn to meet reality halfway."

We at SICR unconditionally guarantee that if you consistently apply the tactics and strategies set forth in this text, it is likely that even the most formal, orthodox Freudian will one day put down his notepad, give you a hearty clap on the back, join you on the couch, and confide, "Let's hurry this up so we can get together with the wives."

An Amazing X Ray of
the Human Unconscious—
The SICR Scale

You aren't neurotic because of a lack of brains or a constitutional deficiency. In most instances, self-pity, self-abasement, or self-indulgence are hard at work and have robbed you of your normal judgment and common sense. The bottom line is, "Do you have enough of a healthy core remaining to be able to turn your neurosis to your advantage?"

In order to find out whether you have the right stuff to become one of your analyst's personal favorites, we at SICR have developed a powerful personality screening device. If you answer these questions honestly, our experts can instantly ascertain whether you have a smart unconscious or a lost cause. Over 73 percent of those applicants who passed the test were able to find a permanent place in some fortunate analyst's practice.

Simply answer yes or no. Delusions don't count and auditory hallucinations will immediately disqualify you.

Give yourself one point for every "no" answer and find your rating:

If you score 0 through 5, call 911 and tell them to come immediately. Your early childhood experiences have gotten the best of you, and for some reason they've all come out of the closet at the same time.

If you score 6 through 14, you probably had at least one parent who treated you decently, and you do a fairly good job of masking your disturbance in public. If you commit yourself to long-term intensive treatment with a highly qualified professional, you may yet lead a normal life.

If you score 15 through 20, you are a prize prospect and are eligible for a SICR scholarship. You have it in you to be the envy of the waiting-room crowd and can enliven the monotony of an analyst's practice for years to come. Your case and its associated symptoms can become a byword for neurosis at its entertaining best. Your latest breakthrough may well be to announce to your analyst that you're divorcing your wife and marrying your computer.

THE SICR SCALE

1. I always keep myself aloft.
2. I am sure that medical science will in time wipe out childish diseases.
3. No one is listening.
4. The other line always moves faster than mine.
5. It's usually the wrong time of the month.
6. I prefer to get my orgasms out of the way.
7. I have difficulty remembering how many children I have.
8. Nothing succeeds like failure.
9. I'd rather go to a full-service than a self-service analyst.
10. Nothing is my fault.
11. The only disease I had as a child I think my mother invented.
12. Some paranoids have enemies.
13. I consider most fun to be a total waste of time.
14. I rarely ingest food or drink.
15. I never show a Doberman Pinscher that I'm afraid.
16. If someone stuck me with a pin, it would not hurt.
17. I don't like to wear clothes when I'm around people.
18. I can't stand reading a newspaper that someone else has read first.
19. All babies look like little monkeys.
20. Bagels make me nervous.

The Odds are 3 to 1 That You're Hopeless

If you don't want to take unnecessary chances, you might want to consult the chart below for the odds against being helped by psychoanalysis. Based on the latest computer information from Las Vegas, in some cases psychoanalysis isn't a good bet.

Common kvetch	100–1 Losing proposition.
Rebel without a clue	90–1
Phobic about elephants	80–1 Too big a neurosis to fit in the office.
Chronic lecher	75–1 Familiarity breeds attempt.
"Psychosemitic" diseases: Trumbernick Schlemiel Schlemazel Schmeggege Schmendrick Schlepp	 50–1
Paranoid character	30–40–1 Depends on whether it's his friends or enemies chasing after him.
The obsessive (arrested for doing the wave in church)	20–1 Person #1: He hasn't been himself lately. Person #2: Let's hope he stays that way.
Anxiety neurotic	15–1
Hysterical patient	5–1 Adds sex and spice to analytic drama. Unless it's a male patient, in which case shock therapy is advisable.

Factors That Influence the Psychoanalyst's Decision to Go Into Early Retirement

A recent survey of 760 psychoanalysts was conducted to determine at what age they plan to retire, and to identify what factors might motivate them to prolong their clinical careers. Nearly 53 percent of the analysts interviewed anticipated retiring by age 70 because of "patient fatigue," 30 percent intimated that they plan to work beyond 70, and a surprising 13.5 percent reported that they plan to practice psychoanalysis for two years after they die.

With regard to this latter group, the general consensus was that they "were just getting the hang of it" and it would be a shame to waste all those years of experience just because they were dead.

Passing the Sniff Test

The analyst Harry Stack Sullivan had a dog who was an expert at sniffing between the lines. Sullivan kept the dog with him behind the couch for differential diagnoses. If a patient was evasive or acted suspiciously, the dog would start growling. This alerted Sullivan to the fact that he might be overlooking something and prompted him to make his famous quip, "Two heads are always better than one."

Freud also made use of his dog in the office. In the middle of a session with a particularly resistant patient, Freud would turn to his Chow, Shatsi, and say, "I think it's all right for you to go now. It doesn't look as though this is going anywhere anyway." With patients who were late with their payments, Freud let his dog out into the waiting room as a bill collector.

My best advice is to bring a bone, pack a steak, or, if you're caught empty-handed, lie on your back, raise your legs and arms and show that you mean no harm. If you pass the sniff test, it means you're an okay guy.

What the Good Patient Should Be Ready to Provide

- News bulletins from the outside world
- The weather for the weekend
- The new "in" places
- Instructions for programming a VCR
- Good housekeepers
- Names of reliable handymen and home contractors
- Wholesale outlets
- Good restaurants
- An appealing, infectious good humor
- Honest, inexpensive auto mechanics
- Medical specialists who make home visits
- A clear explanation of frequent-flyer miles
- Nice getaway places and weekend retreats
- Travel bargains
- The advantages of leasing versus buying cars
- Gossip about celebrities
- Real estate steals and bank foreclosures
- Up-to-date movie and theater reviews
- Tennis tips
- Copies of expensive computer software
- Help with plans for a forthcoming wedding or Bar Mitzvah.
- Advice about diets that work
- The very latest from *Prevention Magazine* (e.g., mayonnaise is good for your hair; cholesterol is actually healthy)

Always keep a pair of pliers and a screwdriver handy. Offer to repair your analyst's appliances, change washers in the faucets, clean water drains in the sink and toilet, rake the leaves in his backyard, and replace vents and valves on the radiator. Bring a quill pen and offer to address the invitations to his daughter's wedding while you chat. (Learn calligraphy first.) You'll be pleasantly surprised at how much this will help the analyst look kindly upon you.

CHAPTER II

How to Choose an Analyst Who Can Love You

When working toward the solution of a problem, it always
helps if you already know the answer.

OTTO RANK

S ICR views the selection process as a crucial preliminary
step toward becoming the most favored patient. Chemistry,
compatibility, and credentials are uppermost considerations, of
course, but in the end, certain intangible factors like valet
parking, location, and the analyst's height can make all the
difference.*

Knowing Your Choices

You probably will want to inquire about the analyst's background, training, and orientation. Just don't let your death
instinct get the better of you by asking whether he is a "real"
doctor or only a psychologist. The California courts have ruled
that this is justifiable grounds for homicide.

Many mental health professionals offer similar services.
Here is a guide:

---

*Sigmund Freud was five-feet eight-inches tall, which is about the
right height for an analyst sitting down. Any analyst over six-feet-tall has
his head in the clouds and is going to overlook those small important
details, and should be suspect.

• **Psychiatrist.** The only mental health professional with a medical degree (which he will mention at least seventeen times in the very first hour). This is a man who had an early and violently fearful reaction to blood and a concomitant attraction to large sums of money, but was not astute enough to pick dermatology. His wife and children know enough to call him "Doctor."

Without a stethoscope and white coat, the psychiatrist often feels naked and unarmed. His first line of defense is medication. Since most sensible neurotics object to being sedated or tranquilized, the psychiatrist becomes an expert at persuading people to take medications for their own good. Somewhat more sophisticated psychiatrists try to follow M. Romer's advice, "Look smart, say nothing, and mumble a lot in German." It is for this reason that it's sometimes difficult to distinguish competent from incompetent psychiatrists. The best advice is to listen for a higher-level mumble with an occasional well-placed Freudian grunt.

• **Psychologist.** He is usually a Ph.D. who has for years looked forward to being able to call up restaurants and make reservations by saying, "This is Dr...." He always uses his title but still feels kind of funny about it.

Early in his career he thought he would be an experimental psychologist and work with rats, but, he changed his mind when his wife wouldn't let him touch her. If a psychologist ever asks you for "money," he probably graduated from an unaccredited program. One of the major benefits of earning an advanced degree is that he is permitted to charge a "fee." Only plumbers ask for money. If he's on the humanistic side, he'll gravitate toward a homey, informal office atmosphere and chat with you "off the record" at the beginning of each session about how the weekend was out in the Hamptons. His main competitive sport is keeping his weight down.

• **Psychoanalyst.** In the good old days, it was easy enough to recognize a classical psychoanalyst by his beard and his pipe. When tennis became de rigueur for analysts, however, many shed their beards so they could observe their backhands in action.

Ever since smoking made them bad role models for their patients, analysts have been unhappily deprived of their pipes as well. Not only has this made them cranky, but they also seem less profound without the habit of fiddling with their stems or stroking their beards while they frantically dream up a pithy thought or two.

Analysts seem more interested in deeper problems and hidden meanings than the other mental health practitioners. This insatiable need to search between the lines can make an analyst sound stuffy and academic when all he wants to know is what the heck is really going on. Between you and me, the psychoanalyst is someone who doesn't understand people but is paid to try. (Of course the analyst can't ever admit this; otherwise you'll wonder what you're paying him for.) Oscar Wilde once said, "Only superficial people need to look beneath the surface." Of course you can't say this directly. That would only hurt his feelings. Still, you could have a dream in which one of the characters says, "Beware lest you lose the substance by grasping at the shadow."

Within the field of analysis itself, there are several different schools to choose from besides the classic Freudian. These include:

• **Adlerian.** The followers of Alfred Adler are usually short, stout men who wear brown suits and believe that most neuroses stem from man's need to compensate for sexual organ inferiorities. The analysis usually consists of endless hours of sifting through your unconscious for evidence of a relentless search for power, prestige, fame, and wealth. If your ordinary life is extremely dull, this may provide some much needed excitement.

• **Existentialism.** Existential analysts focus on helping patients find personal meaning and spiritual significance in the unimportant events of daily life. If you're interested in worrying about something different than most of your friends, this form of treatment is worth considering.

KURT A. ADLER

• **Gestalt Therapy.** This treatment, developed by Fritz Perls, focuses on the individual getting his feelings out by yelling at chairs and hitting cushions and anything else that won't fight back. When treatment is over, the patient can feel comfortable and well adjusted in any room full of furniture.

• **Jungian.** The writings and theories of Carl Jung are so filled with mysticism and a search for the soul that no one, not even analysts, understand them. If you want to spend a few hours each week in the pleasant company of an intelligent man who scratches his head and debates with himself about whether you've discovered your soul yet, this analysis is guaranteed not to have too jarring an effect on your daily life.

• **Family Therapy.** A form of treatment in which the entire family gets collective blame for your troubles. If you want to see your parents without having to eat dinner with them each and every Friday, this approach may be appealing.

Advanced Hugging

Many contemporary analysts employ certain extra-analytic techniques—in some instances marked deviations from standard procedures—to gain additional therapeutic leverage. A course on the hug is now taught in many analytic programs.

Among the approaches taught are the hello hug (friendly but open-ended), the goodbye hug (firm and sincere), the loving hug (affectionate but not erotic; the lower part of the bodies never touch), the long hug (conveys support and empathy) and the joyful hug (celebrating a breakthrough or special event). Analysts who for religious reasons do not engage in hugging, take alternative courses like "The Twenty-seven Variations on the Use of Benevolent Neutrality as a Technique."

A Beach-Blanket View of the Analysts

An investigative reporter for the Style section of the *New York Times* discovered that analysts meet in little discussion circles at their various vacation retreats to swap war stories and catch up on the latest approaches. What is most important for your purposes, however, is that you can learn a lot about what kind of analyst is right for you by wandering the beaches. What began as an informal spontaneous gathering has now become far more complicated. The *Times* reporter gained access to a classified map of beach blankets at the various resorts on the East Coast where analysts assemble. These blankets contain no easily identifiable marks, but analysts from the various schools are given secret codes to find their way to the right place. For example, the field of green blankets to the left of the ice cream stand in Truro is a hotbed of arguing Kleinians. The purple blanket to the left of the restrooms in Amagansett is home to a bunch of Jungians trying to find their shadows. Over the dune to the right is a volleyball game. Usually the sides are equally divided up, Neo-Freudians versus classical analysts. If you're any good, they do accept ringers.

SICR is now selling reprints of these maps ($5.00 each) to eligible patients. In a bathing suit, the average patient can usually pass for an analyst. Just don't say anything that will give you away. Hang around, listen in, and in September you'll know which blanket you'll want to pull over your face during your analysis.

Telephone Tips and Tactics

Your initial contact with an analyst will be by phone. If you keep getting a busy signal or an unfriendly recording, take the hint and try another analyst. If you were referred by a close friend, don't think you're being paranoid if you suspect that he or she undermined you during a session in an unconscious fit of sibling rivalry. Nevertheless, a personal recommendation is probably the best way to find an analyst. It's hard to be totally convinced, though, when someone says, "This guy is great. I've been seeing him three times a week for ten years." The analyst's answering machine has probably been programmed to carefully screen out people with your type of neurosis anyway. Don't make a pest of yourself.

The best time to call is precisely ten to the hour, just when

Classified Information
on
Amagansett Beach, August 1993

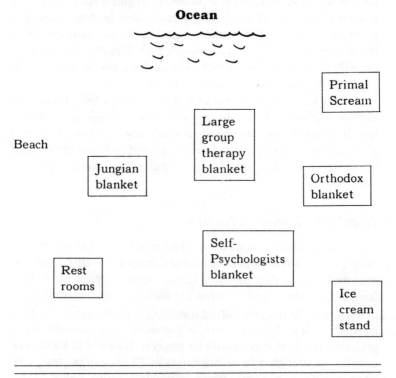

August Blanket Topics—Week of August 17

Jungians	What color is your mantra?
Orthodox Freudians	Dare one hate his patients?
Self-Psychologists	This blanket is occupied by only one person at a time.
Primal Screamers	Each person will tell a patient war story and then scream for as long as he wants.
Group Therapy blanket	Mostly used to recruit people for the volleyball game.

---

the analyst is concluding his session. If you think of yourself as seriously committed, it might be a good investment to purchase a timepiece marketed by Freud Toy Inc., sold exclusively to compulsive neurotics. This watch is synchronized with Vienna Mean Time and beeps precisely at 10:50, 11:50, 12:50 and so on, Monday through Friday, except during the month of August. Most analysts have another version made by Rolex that runs a little faster. A recent innovation is the forty-five-minute hour, which was introduced by fast-track analysts with Swatch watches who have larger portfolios and dabble in options.

Try to sound upbeat, hopeful, and disarming. Don't be a fool and let your unconscious give you away. "He who has eyes to see and ears to hear becomes convinced that mortals can keep no secret. If their lips are silent, they gossip with their fingertips; betrayal oozes its way through every pore" (Freud, 1923). Save any mention of your more exotic out-of-body experiences and past lives till much later, when you've gained his confidence. Also, certain certain white lies are okay in the very beginning. Don't make the same mistake as the patient who admitted right off the bat that he had administered the

Heimlich maneuver to four people who didn't need it—the analyst will be afraid to be in the same room with you.

Speak clearly and without hesitation. Don't breathe too heavily and try not to perspire. You'll only get the analyst unnecessarily nervous. You have about thirty seconds before your neurosis starts to sound vaguely familiar and the analyst's unresolved fear of strangers begins to alert him.* Finally, never makes the mistake of informing the analyst that you found him through the Yellow Pages. He will either think you are a serial killer or conclude that your husband is in the Mafia.

Where Your Analyst's Referrals Come From

Wrong numbers	6%
Professional reputation	7%
Personal appearance on the *Howard Stern Show*, articles about him in *Playboy*, *People Magazine*, etc.	14%
Chapters and articles in books and journals	6%
Speeches to lay groups, appearances at analytic societies and symposiums	17%
Recommendations by colleagues, associates, supervisees, friends, neighbors, relatives	10%
Enthusiastic word of mouth by satisfied patients distributing analyst's cards at toll plazas, Madison Square Garden, Wall Street at lunchtime, and the World Trade Center	40%

---

*This has come to be known as déjà vu. The analyst is haunted by the memory of having been traumatized by someone similar to you in the remote past.

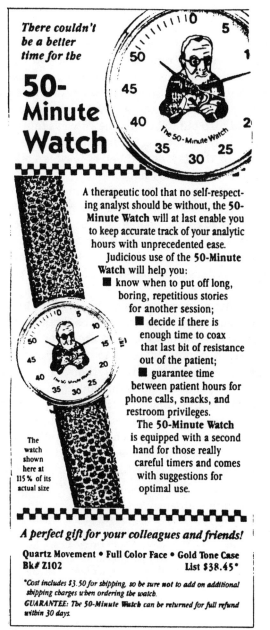

There couldn't be a better time for the

50- Minute Watch

A therapeutic tool that no self-respecting analyst should be without, the **50-Minute Watch** will at last enable you to keep accurate track of your analytic hours with unprecedented ease. Judicious use of the **50-Minute Watch** will help you:

■ know when to put off long, boring, repetitious stories for another session;

■ decide if there is enough time to coax that last bit of resistance out of the patient;

■ guarantee time between patient hours for phone calls, snacks, and restroom privileges.

The **50-Minute Watch** is equipped with a second hand for those really careful timers and comes with suggestions for optimal use.

The watch shown here at 115% of its actual size

A perfect gift for your colleagues and friends!

Quartz Movement • Full Color Face • Gold Tone Case
Bk# Z102   List $38.45*

*Cost includes $3.50 for shipping, so be sure not to add on additional shipping charges when ordering the watch.
GUARANTEE: The 50-Minute Watch can be returned for full refund within 30 days.

COURTESY OF *FREUD TOY, INC.*

Make Him Want You

Every analyst needs strong reassurance that you won't be a blot on his professional reputation and that you will represent him well in the community. He doesn't want to have to worry that people will remark, "She's even worse off since she went to see Dr. So-and-So." Offer the analyst some reason to believe that you could turn out to be what he's always fantasized about: a stunning analytic success, a fascinating case, a cheerful interlude during the day, or at the very least, an opportunity to build an extension onto his house.

Over time, analysts become tired and disillusioned. This makes them particularly prone to the more contagious neuroses. They already have enough depression and agita in their lives, why do they need more?* If the analyst sizes you up as one great big headache, he will tell you his hours are filled and refer you to a colleague he never liked, one who specializes in "losers."

Try to enlist his confidence by letting him know right off that you realize you're in for the long haul but that you have a highly cooperative unconscious and are determined to finally listen to reason. Analysts tend to favor patients who are psychologically minded and think there is a psychosomatic basis for just about everything, including the common cold. Confide in the analyst that you firmly believe in the unconscious roots of tennis elbow ("The arm bone's connected to the head bone"). If you're a hypochondriac, tell him that your mother had a walk-in medicine chest and he'll smile. Most analysts prefer a note of cheerful pessimism to grim optimism

---

*By this time, you've probably heard of the organization, Analysts Anonymous. This support group has a membership that consists of analysts who swore that they would only carry a case load of thirty-five patients, tops. When the thirty-sixth patient calls, before the analyst gives in to his addiction and fills yet another hour, he calls his buddy, who helps him stick to his plan. This same system has helped many an analyst get through particularly bad days, when too many patients start off the session with, "I've got nothing to say..."

and despite their disclaimers would prefer it if you were only selectively candid.

Quickly move to establish the depth of your interest and sincerity with simple, direct statements. "Do you think five sessions a week are enough? My insurance covers everything"; "I have two uncles and a cousin who also want to come to you"; I don't mind coming any time of the day or night. Just fit me in at your convenience"; "Do you mind if I pay in cash?"

If he is still hesitant, establish that you are not suicidal unless pushed, have a lurid and intriguing sexual history to tell, will negotiate on symptoms, and already have a booking to discuss your problem on *Geraldo*, *Sally Jesse Raphael* and the *Oprah Winfrey Show*.

Keep in mind that a recent survey of over 3,000 analysts revealed that the major criteria they use to determine a good analytic candidate are:

1. Intelligent enough to concede a point
2. No insurance forms to fill out
3. Doesn't argue about paying for missed appointments
4. Neuroses that make sense
5. Ability to afford three or more sessions per week
6. A high capacity for independently coming to the same conclusion as the analyst

---

Why Your Analyst Really Wants to Help You

Seventeen hundred psychoanalysts were polled about what prompted them to go into the profession. One hundred sixty-nine said they liked to help people, and two hundred eighty-nine said their mothers had told them, "It is a cruel world out there," so they thought they would be better off having an indoor job. The remainder were not reluctant to admit that "it was one of the only times in my life that someone listened to what I had to say."

7. A great body and terrific legs

8. At the conclusion of the session, let him use the bathroom first.

Some of these qualities may be difficult to convey in a brief chat over the phone. Offer to send the analyst notarized copies of your Dunn & Bradstreet rating, letters of recommendation from your last three employers, and a color photo of yourself in a bathing suit.

Sigmund Freud's Advice to the Analyst Considering Going Into Private Practice

Be mature
Be diplomatic.
Get a son-in-law who is a creative accountant.
Be punctual.
Be available.
Get nice people for patients.
Get your landlord into treatment and sign a long lease.
Be flexible.
Have self-restraint.
Marry a woman who is a good decorator.
Have your waiting room radio dialed to mellow FM.

The impossible task of keeping all of these things in mind while remembering to water the plants and keep up with the bills causes many an analyst to feel overwhelmed. In fact, the most popular magazine that analysts subscribe to is the *Headache Journal* and the most common occupational disorders are TMJ, the growling stomach reaction, and irritable bowel syndrome.

CHAPTER III

How to Interpret Your Analyst's Interior Designs

Trust your own healthy neurotic instincts. You have conjured a picture of an analyst in your mind and you should not settle for less. The sort of uncomfortable nervousness that Woody Allen* made famous, with a nice sense of humor, is a good starting point and can lead God knows where.

It has been scientifically proven that bearded, nearsighted, slightly overweight analysts with names of eight or more letters and warm brown eyes, with a certain world-weary, rumpled appearance, dressed in tweed jackets and baggy pants, with Central European accents, have far more character and soul than fastidious anal-retentives. If you don't catch the drift of what such an analyst is saying, it doesn't matter. What does matter is that he understands you. It probably wasn't intended for your ears anyhow; that's why he speaks with an accent. Be sure he wears horn-rimmed glasses; otherwise how would you know that he keeps up with the literature?

Would you really trust an analyst with an anglicized name in a blue suit who looks like William Buckley or George Plimpton to understand the pain and suffering you went through when your sister (aged two) ate your stamp collection, or that you didn't notice until it was too late that your mother continued taking baths with you until you were fourteen? How can you ever explain to a sterile buttoned-down doctor whose worst problem was deciding which prep school to go to the guilt and shame you feel because you never masturbated like all the

---

*Now we know it was for good reason.

other kids on the block and that when you finally did get around to it, your penis turned black? Can you expect someone with thin lips and a formal manner to grasp the utter humiliation you felt when your mother insisted on heating your ice cream because she didn't want you to get a chill, and when she took you to the girls' bathroom because it was warmer there?

The Office

Once you have looked the doctor over, scan his quarters.* Two walls' worth of credentials and diplomas are a minimum requirement. Look for grade school and high school diplomas. See if he has a certificate confirming that he was captain of his team in Color War. If they are all prominently displayed, the analyst suffered early trauma and is deeply insecure but is an all-around good guy. Call him Herr Professor and it will probably strike just the right chord.

The Analytic Couch

The couch should be reasonably lumpy, with a few broken springs to betray a busy practice, years of experience, and an analyst who doesn't value form over substance. Behind the couch, look for an Eames chair that adjusts to a doze position if necessary.

At some time early in treatment, the analyst will invite you to lie on the couch. This is not a proposition; he is only being classical.

It is a popular myth that the analytic couch was introduced merely to help patients gain access to their deepest unconscious through free association. Rather, there is strong evidence that Freud couldn't stand being stared at eight hours a day. He could not properly concentrate on Oedipal wishes, fetishes,

---

*Don't take a cuckoo clock personally. Some analysts have the bad habit of falling into a very deep sleep. If the clock didn't wake them, they could be late for the next patient.

An impressive wall full of diplomas is an absolute must for any analyst's office. In the picture on the left the author poses with Otto Spinholtz. This remarkable man closely resembled Theodor Reik, an early associate of Freud's. For $125 a picture, he made a good living, traveling around the country with his white laboratory coat, adding luster and prestige to many an analyst's office.

American Express features a special card for paranoids. Even though it is their hour, they are afraid that unless they reserve the couch in advance, the analyst will give it away.

anal fixations, and the like without feeling terribly self-conscious.

It occurred to Freud that if he could sit comfortably well out of view, he could make out his monthly bills, read his mail, keep up with his voluminous correspondence, and still give the patient his undivided attention. It was during this period of enlightenment that Freud first earned his reputation as a good listener.

The Analytic Chair

Whether an analyst uses an Eames lounge chair, the Saar Womb Chair, or a director's chair, never sit in it uninvited, even as a joke. Remember what Poppa Bear said. If a man's home is his castle, a man's chair is his throne. The analyst's chair gives him a reassuring sense of power and authority. When he sits behind the couch and settles back with the pad on his lap, he feels just like Freud. One analyst, Wilhelm Stekel, was so impressed by the wisdom granted him by the authority of his chair that he sometimes asked selected patients whether he could swap places with them and lie on the couch. He would get into his own stream of consciousness, get some helpful advice from the patient, and then calmly say, "Okay, let's try not to forget who we are." Without another word being said, he would rise and change back to being the analyst.

The Bookshelves

Be sure to check the bookshelves, and look for a bust of Freud somewhere. There should be many dusty, dog-eared books, piles of moldy unread journals with the word "international" in their titles, a sprinkling of pop psychology books, and no texts under three hundred pages in length (the thicker the books, the deeper the analyst). In order to rest assured that the analyst knows what he's doing, discreetly take note of whether the twenty-six volume *Standard Edition of the Collected Works of Sigmund Freud* in the original German (light green cover) is on the top shelf. Then see whether he keeps up with more recent developments in the field and has the fifteen-volume work, *The Psychotherapy Finances in Private Practice*.

The Consulting Room

The consulting room should breathe a wholly unapologetic eclecticism. Ideally, it should have a cozy, comforting, "lived-in" atmosphere. The ghosts of unresolved neurotic complexes hover everywhere. The various mementos and objects d'art should reflect the spirit of the analyst and the people who frequent the room.* Your intimate familiarity with all of its

---

*Some analysts go a bit too far in "making a statement." We see Mr. and and Mrs. L., who were patients of Dr. R. Dr. R. arranged to have them stuffed and mounted after ten years of unsuccessful treatment.

The Analytic Couch. During World War II, the government issued silhouette charts of enemy aircraft so the populace could distinguish friend from foe at a glance. The following photographs of a representative group of analytic couches will save you the embarrassment of having to ask your analyst what school of thought he follows. (Analysts tend to get testy and mutter "eclectic" under their breath.) Study these photos carefully and you'll soon know whether you're in the right place.

REPRODUCTION OF ANALYTIC COUCHES COURTESY OF IMPERIAL LEATHER CO.

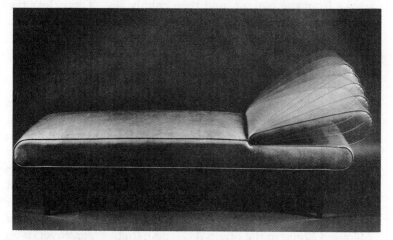

The Jungian Couch. The large extrovert model. The couch expands to accommodate much thrashing about, grandiose egos, and severely overinflated forms of narcissism.

The Adlerian Couch. This couch is built small for patients with gross organ inferiorities. This is in keeping with Alfred Adler's historic pronouncement, "The small penis means nothing compared to the rest of life."

The Object Relations Couch. The most contemporary, "cutting edge" school of psychoanalysis. This approach specializes in treating patients who are overly attached to inanimate objects. The absence of close, intimate relationships in early childhood has led to an emotional displacement onto "things." This infantile fixation onto fax machines, BMW's and high-tech sneakers is among the most difficult neuroses to treat. The object relations couch, with its stark simplicity of design, cold cushion, and hard pillow, is intended to bring the patient back to the barren, stark environment that he is most familiar with.

The Self-Psychology Couch. This couch was expressly designed by Heinz Kohut to treat holdovers from the "me" generation. This neurotic subgroup regressed to a point of self-centered narcissism to compensate for the traumatic experience of having just missed being a baby boomer. The analyst must be prepared to deal with the patient's shocking realization that he is not the only person to lie on the couch. This model should be fitted with lots of pillows and bolsters to provide the patient with the empathy and support he needs.

Few observers today remember the meteoric short-lived popularity of the Climax Couch. Once analysis became popular in Vienna, it was brought to America in 1912. Soon the competition for analytic patients became so fierce that analysts made extravagant promises to their patients. One group of analysts promised an insight every hour. Another group of psychoanalysts went still further, appealing to the large number of sexual dysfunctionals out there and promising them a crescendo if not a climax every session.

details will heighten your feeling of security and repose. See if you can spot any autographed photos of celebrities ("To someone who has changed my life") or framed testimonials from cured patients.

This window into the person of the analyst can enrich your understanding of his reality. Pictures of his family members and close friends, tennis trophies (earned or bought), mounted gun collections, souvenirs of places visited and gladly remembered, etchings, pieces of sculpture, and cans of Mace comprise a little world that reflects deliberate choices.

The Waiting Room

Despite its reputation for gaiety, turn-of-the-century Vienna was a very closed-minded, provincial society. Thus, when Freud began his clinical practice, he had to make very sure that his patients would not have to risk malicious gossip and exposure by walking through a full waiting room. They were always shown out another door, thus avoiding the posssible embarrassment of meeting by chance someone they knew.

Analysts today who follow the classical tradition frequently practice from split-level houses in the suburbs. (Occasionally we now see the interesting spectacle of an exiting patient falling from the second story into the analyst's rose bushes.) In big cities, the emergence of group practices in which analysts share a common suite of offices has given the waiting room some new cachet.

Faith Popcorn, the chairwoman of the Brain Reserve, a Manhattan trend research firm who styles herself a Nostradamus of popular culture, says that Egonomics is now the name of the game. Analysts on Manhattan's Upper East Side, for example, compete to be the most popular in-spot for singles. In fact, the *Zagat Restaurant Guide* recently published a supplement that rates New York analysts' waiting rooms for atmosphere, bathroom facilities, congenial company, and decor. One highly successful practitioner provides a pool table, light refreshments, and soft music. Word has it that when it's

The modern psychoanalyst must strike a balance between discrete anonymity and a positive role model. If you discover yourself taking an interest in tennis and developing a backhand even without owning a racquet, it shows that analysis is taking hold. If you begin harboring a nostalgic attitude toward the old Brooklyn Dodgers even though you never went to Ebbets Field, a still deeper level of your psyche is being reached.

time for the session to begin, many patients actually have to be coaxed into finishing up their networking and hurrying their goodbyes. Not to be outdone, the chic analysts on the West Side serve pâté from Zabar's, have sing-alongs, and throw some of the best parties at holiday time.

Something to take note of is that some analysts cheat. They play such melancholy music in the waiting room that you'd have to be psychotic not to get depressed. Social scientists have proven that patients susceptible to these subliminal cues not only tend to open up more, but are more likely to ask for extra sessions each week. It's one thing listening to Lithium 100, but "Rainy Days and Mondays," "Killing Me Softly," "Never Gonna Fall in Love," and Megadeth's Greatest Hits are going too far.

There is another, more cynical school of thought, that the waiting room should be viewed in a more sinister light—as a simmering cauldron of primitive passion crowded full of congenital yentas whose death wishes toward hated siblings are not the exception but the rule.* It is suggested that beneath the thin veneer of civility and politeness lies a deep residue of possessiveness, suspicion, and distrust. It would not be an exaggeration to assume that each of those seated sees you as a loathsome pretender to their privileged position as the favorite. If the patients happen to be waiting to see another analyst, they will often give you a look that says, "My analyst can see right through your analyst." Remember Freud's words well. "It is as perilous to win one's Oedipal battles as to lose them."† Even paranoids have enemies.

---

*A yenta is a real blabbermouth, malicious gossip.

†The "thinking man's neurotic" will lay the proper groundwork for success as soon as he enters the analyst's building. Give the doorman a generous present for Christmas and make pleasant small talk with people in the elevator. This way, they'll be sure to pass the word on to the analyst's wife that looks can be deceiving and compared to the others, you're not as bad as you look. Mumbling "Apartment 4C" won't let you off the hook. Everybody knows what kind of people get off on the fourth floor.

Since everything you do is suspect, don't even try to introduce friendly icebreakers. "What are you in for?" will undoubtedly be taken the wrong way and even something as tactful as "So, what's your problem?" is subject to misinterpretation. Anything, even any reasonable question, is seen as prying. Leave them guessing about who you are and what you're there for. Don't borrow the sports column or even ask about the time. Treachery abounds everywhere; every unguarded move that you make will be rejected and duly reported to the analyst to undercut you.

One cardinal rule: never make eye contact. Every single patient in the waiting room is barely controlling the impulse to devour you, poison you, choke you, chop you into little pieces, drain and castrate you. Their desires to distort your friendly gestures should not be minimized.

Also watch out for a new strain of waiting-room neurotic, the gossip dyslexic. They talk in front of other people's backs. Perhaps the best approach to take is an air of cool intimidation. If you can't look like Clint Eastwood, try to appear nonchalant, as though their common concerns are not your own—play the role of a colleague of the doctor, waiting for him to complete his work so the two of you can go out to lunch. Humming something like Marky Mark's "Good Vibrations" sets the right tone. Choose something bouncy and upbeat. Your very bearing will insinuate that you had a healthier childhood than they did. If you're sure there's nobody around, and you've already been diagnosed as a psychopath, turn down the volume of the radio and eavesdrop on the previous patient. Maybe you can learn something from his mistakes.

The Magazine Rack

Notice the magazine rack. The *National Geographic* shows that the analyst is a solid, respectable sort who can be counted on to spend your money for legitimate travel purposes. A subscription to *Spike*, a magazine for foot fetishists, shows he caters to special interests. *Playboy* is designed to demonstrate that he's

You can live days without food and water
but only seconds without air—oxygen
which is 21% of fresh air you breathe.
PUSH OUT YOUR THIRD VEST BUTTON
breathe deeply—be oxygenated—be energized
a powerful producer

If the other people in the waiting room are reacting casually to this totally paranoid picture, get out and don't look back. The analyst treats only very disturbed individuals who seem to understand the deeper meaning of this picture.

hip and that you should feel free to talk about ménage à trois, tantric orgasms, enlarging your G spot, or your latest sexual positions without fear of embarrassment. If you're paranoid, be suspicious if he still subscribes to *Psychology Today* even though it has been out of print for three years. He might not want you to know what analysts are really saying behind your back. If you see copies of *Fortune* or *Business Week*, hope that the analyst invests in growth stocks and that the market is up. *Glamour, Self, Vogue, Mademoiselle, Allure*, and *Mirabella* show that even if he's a man, he at least has a passing knowledge of women's issues.

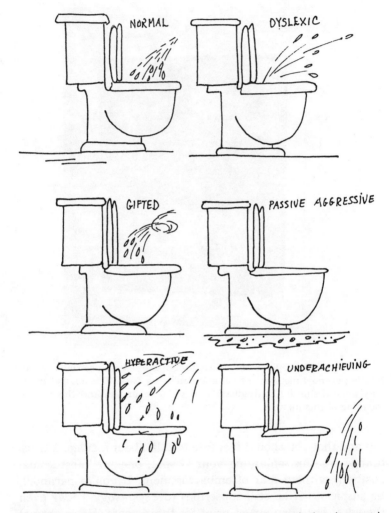

It is common knowledge that one's capacity for genital excitement is closely interwoven with the pride one takes in one's urinary stream. In some cases, the temptation to enjoy the pleasure of sinking floating objects in the toilet bowl becomes a perversion if it seems far more interesting than having sex.

Freud later came to believe that the fact that little girls couldn't participate in the same kind of fun was far worse than penis envy in determining their cruel fate.

The Decor

Check the decor. Be alert to wilted plants, fish floating belly up in the tank, and needlepoint samplers with sentiments like "Life is a bitch and then you die." If the analyst's cat or dog is color-coordinated with the furnishings, beware—you may be in the hands of a degenerate. The same is true of perverted analysts who believe in bestiality disguised as "Stress Management for Pets." You might get scratched or bitten in the waiting room.

The Two-Bathroom Office

A recent study directly challenges Freudian theory regarding the infantile roots of neurosis. New research boldly suggests that the hidden basis for most emotional problems is that many crowded households have only a single bathroom. The lack of privacy, the desperate power struggles, the competition for who goes first and what takes priority, the banging on the door—this is stress with nothing subtle about it.

In light of these findings, certain innovations are being experimented with, so far with very surprising results. Analysts who have two bathrooms adjoining the waiting room report a significant improvement in the stress level of their patients. Several analysts have even introduced a radical approach. They have two bathrooms but the patient never gets to see the analyst. This hardly seems to matter. These patients seem to get better also. Patients find that having an oasis of peace and quiet in midtown Manhattan, where they can read the paper at their leisure with nobody hounding them to hurry up, is a turning point in their lives.

Chapter IV

Being "The Good Hour"

Be not afraid of greatness.
WILLIAM SHAKESPEARE

Oedipus, Schoedipus

As Lord Houghten said, "Great thoughts, great feelings came to him like instincts, unawares." Each and every analytic session offers you innumerable opportunities to stand out from the crowd. All you have to remember is that in baiting a mousetrap with cheese, always leave room for the mouse. Analysts are sick and tired of tanned, beautiful blondes, Yuppie spoiled, and bratty kids.

A good old-fashioned neurotic like yourself, with a little sprucing up, deserves a chance. As long as the analyst likes you, he can overlook practically anything. The ultimate proof of this is the famous case of the Wolf Man, who had the worst assortment of perversions and fixations imaginable. Yet Sigmund Freud excused him at every turn, once even going so far as to say, "Oedipus, Schmoedipus, so long as he loves his mother." All because he knew how to report his symptoms clearly, with enthusiasm and gusto. With this in mind, read the remainder of this manual carefully and see whether by the midstage of treatment, your analyst finally says, "I surrender. You are great!"

The Creative Neurotic

What are the real inside secrets for grabbing the analyst's attention and saving yourself from the oblivion of classical interpretations? Try to prevent the analyst from seeing you as just the six o'clock hour.

Failing that, we at SICR counsel defeated neurotics, "Never give up. You never know what the analyst is shopping around for. Don't be afraid to shock and surprise." One patient that I remember well wore a hat with a different feather to every session. Another patient would unexpectedly drop his pants to show his knee brace because he knew he and the analyst shared a strong interest in athletic injuries. The more extraordinary the act, the harder to ignore or neglect. One patient even made the *Guinness Book of World Records*. Under the topic heading, Most Unique Therapeutic Experience, 1987, is the case of a man whose analyst had an office in his house. A new maid saw the man in the waiting room and misunderstood who he was. Thinking he was a relative, she ushered him upstairs—where the analyst was walking around in his underwear, trying to figure out what to put on. No matter what neurotic handicap this patient came in with, he shared a special moment with the analyst that neither of them would ever forget.

It's one thing if you're a cheerful, naturally gifted neurotic, but as a dumb, garden variety neurotic, what can you do to lift your analyst's spirits and renew his faith in Freud? Sometimes it's not enough to name your dog after him, to offer him an organ transplant, or even to send him a birthday card. The secret resource is your recognition that your analyst needs someone like you very badly. The one thing that he lacks most is a generous, unconditional caring force in his life.

Realizing this can express itself in deeds and achievements far beyond anything you ever thought yourself capable of. The first patient to use a Dust Buster under the analytic couch has already been immortalized by election to the Neurotic Hall of Fame.

Understanding inspirations that lie buried in your neurotic unconscious represents your best chance for standing out from the crowd. At first, your analyst will be overwhelmed by your kindness and concern. Slowly but surely a unique relationship will begin to develop, and the analyst will gratefully give you a full credit for restoring his confidence and self-esteem. Just knowing that he'll be able to escape tedium and routine when he sees you at 4 o'clock that afternoon will make him more pleasant to everybody he sees earlier in the day. Or as E. Metzger used to say, "A variety of nothing is superior to the monotony of something." Just imagine your analyst thinking, "He's a pretty good guy. To know him is to love him."

The Black-Belt Neurotic

Neurotic genius is not some mysterious gift which descends by grace on a small number of the especially blessed. It is a heightened expression of ordinary human faculties. The mark of success, of becoming a human tonic, is to concentrate on the task at hand. Behind concentration is will, behind will is the goal, and behind the goal is desire. Don't be ashamed of your powerful desires. Be selfish, be ruthless, be greedy. Everything that bears on the march to becoming the odds-on winner has to be put into action. Your interest, zest, and enthusiasm are the last chance this analyst has to be rescued from his loneliness. Everyone else in his life has abandoned him and taken him for granted. As Coleridge phrased it so well: "Work without hope draws nectar in a sieve / And hope without an object cannot live." You are that person!

The patient who learns to judiciously supply empathy and "emotional refueling" is a Freudian dream come true, a Black-Belt Neurotic.

Patients who bother to ask, "How do you like your coffee?" and come supplied with a choice of Sweet & Low or Equal make all the difference in the world. Scientific observers have noted that after a session or two with such charismatic patients, wilted analysts perk up and become absorbed once again in the professional task at hand. "The sense of security, protection, and reassurance that this outstanding type of patient affords, makes the analyst unconsciously attached to the patient and crave the state of contentment he feels only when he works with such a special individual." (S. Freud, *Studies In Decaffination* 1929.)

Trade Secrets of the Lovable Neurotic

Now comes the good stuff you've been waiting for. In the interest of mental health, SICR has decided to declassify the trade secrets that fatefully determine whether your analyst regards you with "an inner smile," as a source of infinite delight, or whether he simply "tries to help you." To know what we do not know is the beginning of wisdom. Just remember, God has a few of us to whom He whispers in the ear (Browning), and now it's your chance.

SICR's innovative approach to this entire matter is well represented by Ken Boswell, a former New York Met, who once said, "I'm in a rut. I can't break myself of the habit of swinging up at the ball." Yogi Berra answered, "Then swing down." So let's lay the groundwork by citing the obvious.

• Never talk about miracle cures or short-term therapy that you read about in *People* magazine or in *Reader's Digest*.

• Be sure not to praise your friend's analyst or even mention him by name. Your hostile unconscious may be at work. (Remember, the analyst can't defend himself against unfair comparisons without demeaning himself.) Even successful chiropractic adjustments and acupuncture are off limits also.

• Don't tell your analyst that you went to a seance where all your relatives forgave you.

• Don't show too much interest in EST, biofeedback, UFO's, astral projection, psychokinesis, pyramid power, or water witching. The analyst will think you're spacy and unsuitable for a serious endeavor. If you live in California, however, bring up each of these topics so you can discover how much the analyst and you have in common. Liposuction and face-lift talk is all right so long as you know you're narcissistic and can afford it.

• Don't smoke pot in the waiting room or offer to share a joint. The Woodstock generation has grown up, and besides, the analyst, like Bill Clinton, will never let on that he ever inhaled.

• Don't ask about early-bird specials.

• Don't be so gauche as to suggest you had a happy, unremarkable childhood and close relationships with your siblings or that your parents were not intrusive, rejecting, or manipulative. Conflict is the analyst's meat and potatoes. Normalcy is uninspiring, tedious, and, frankly speaking, depressive. In a quiet moment, reflect on your life. Search out the drama and suspense in the commonplace.

• Don't ask if your analyst will come out in the rain and make house calls like Dr. Marcus Welby.

• Don't spend a session agonizing over choosing between a BMW and a Porsche—unless your bill is paid in full.

• Try to avoid pettiness. If the analyst forgets your appointment entirely and there are two people in the waiting room, make a graceful exit. If the analyst comes ten minutes late, think! Is this the worst thing that has happened to you in the last year?

• Don't offer stock tips unless you have insider information.

• Don't show an overenthusiastic affection or attachment to your previous analyst. One early acknowledgment and several backward glances are permissible.

• Try to bring up the thread of an issue the analyst raised during the previous session. The analyst will be amazed that you were listening after all.

• Ask whether you can videotape your sessions so you can study them to see what you're doing wrong.

• Feel your analyst out for his special interests and raise them as sidebars when you have nothing else to discuss. Hint:

tennis stringing, golf, the pennent race, weak backhands, wide-bodied racquets, skiing, and his or her grandchildren are all time-tested topics.

• Analysts enjoy granting small favors. Ask if there's anything to eat in the refrigerator and whether it's all right to change your appointment time because your daughter's getting married.

• Tell the analyst that you have just informed your wife that you intend to leave your beach house to him in your will.

• Obey the law of minor concessions. Concede as much as possible about every arguable point that arises. Analysts appreciate open-mindedness and flexibility.

• Finally, if the analyst looks a little peaked, invite him out into the waiting room and get all the patients there to get together and give him a group hug. Remember the words of John Paul Getty, "...And the meek shall inherit the earth except for the oil and mineral rights."

With these principles in mind, let's get to work so we can get started making you a household name.

The Greeting

Presenting yourself as an unusually sensitive person begins at the moment of greeting—when the tension is greatest. Sigmund Freud explored the momentous issue of "the first move": "How are we to greet the patient? Should we shake hands with him or is this too revealing...We have to remember that the significance of the handshake is different for different patients. For the hysteric, the handshake may represent a promise; for the obsessional a challenge; for the pathologically narcissistic, it may be an attack."

At this time the analyst is going through an exhausting struggle about whether to be friendly or neutral. When in doubt, follow his lead. If the analyst is more formal and aloof, best mask any natural show of warmth lest he feel he's being shown up. On the other hand, if he acts casual and even smiles a bit, you may smile back and make a friendly tribal gesture.

Some analysts prefer to start off sitting behind a desk armed with a notepad. Don't take it personally. This barrier provides them with the safety and detachment they need for their security. When you've convinced them that you don't really want to bury them alive in a slab of cement, they will usually come out from behind the desk.

Be restrained, Analysts always assume you're being manipulative and have a hidden agenda. Maybe you do.

As treatment progresses, stuffy conventions can be bent. Start by innocently offering a stick of gum or Lifesavers. If the analyst falls into your trap, arrive the next time with a delicious jelly apple. If this works, follow it up with coffee and a prune danish. The analyst will slowly be conditioned to anticipate a little surprise at every session and will unconsciously begin to see you as the Good Humor man or as a human Cracker Jack box. When the two of you get really comfortable with each other, you can order in an occasional pizza with extra cheese. When you notice that the analyst seems to be spending a fair amount of time rehashing memorable meals in his life along with his interpretations, you're probably on the right track.

Locating Your Developmental Arrest Level

"Where there is no classical symptom-formation to indicate the fixation period, the patient's assistance is of the utmost diagnostic as well as prognostic significance." (Sigmund Freud, *The Very, Very Cooperative Patient*, 1911.) Although their conscious attitudes may be beyond reproach, most neurotics are determined to undermine psychoanalysis and demonstrate that it is failing through no fault of their own. Be different. Avoid analytic stalemate by taking stock of yourself. Drop some hints about your fixation point along the way.

Ask for suggestions from friends you respect who are already in analysis, or read a good abnormal psychology text so you won't sound stupid. Your developmental arrest level is the point in your life when you stopped maturing and became totally obnoxious. Here are the most popular:

You are anally retentive if:

- You are spiteful, stubborn, and always want to look at everything "ass-ways backwards."
- You never want to go to the same restaurant or movie as the rest of the group and have the autoerotic compulsion to read while sitting on the toilet.
- Your mother's need to housebreak you at two has created a willful, rebellious nature, and an opposition to anything and everyone (a refusal to do your "doody").
- Most probably, the last book you read was *The Accidental Tsoris.*

You are phallically oriented if:

- You think the average penis has a hard life, believe vaginas have teeth, and feel intense castration anxiety around tall women using vacuum cleaners.
- You often dream of penises, demonstrating a symbolic interest in baseball, warfare, and rocketry, but usually go to sleep early with a night-light on.
- Your favorite book is *She Shtups to Conquer.*

You are orally fixated if:

- You carry cigarettes years after you gave up smoking, want to be tucked in while on the couch, enjoy eating more than you enjoy sex, cry a lot for no reason, are constantly surprised that the analyst has other patients, and dream of him in the guise of a breast, a bottle, or a Twinkie.
- You are proud of your charter membership in the Clean Plate Club and bore all of your friends with talk about your cholesterol level and "cleaning out your system."
- Your favorite book is *To Have and Have Nosh.*

You are polymorphous perverse if:

- You have a weird collection of symptoms that make absolutely no sense at all and provide the clinical picture of a perfectly pointless neurosis.
- Your search for meaning leads you to believe that you lived a previous life as a dog. If the analyst calls your bluff and asks you to identify your breed, you get insulted, think he's talking down to you, and start barking.
- Your favorite books are *The Big Shlep* and *Matzoh Do About Nothing*.

Choosing the Right Problem

Sometime during the early sessions you are expected to tell the analyst your whole unhappy history. The ideal presenting problem is one that the analyst knows how to cure but requires a great deal of time to work on.

When choosing a problem, try to stay abreast of chic neuroses. If a neurosis has been mentioned in *Cosmo* or *Vanity Fair* three times in a year, it's no longer considered obscure; it's fashionably correct.

No one has inferiority complexes anymore—they suffer from low self-esteem. Nervousness is out, anxiety is boring, but everyone suffers from stress and burnout. There's practically nothing new to be said about intimacy problems unless you take a really novel approach. One woman who was struggling with the fear of giving in to positive feelings made the sort of Freudian slip that could make an analyst's career. She told her lover, "Go away nearer." Another patient was fearful of being possessed by love. She said, "It is as if a person in jail becomes panicky at the thought of being arrested." Who could resist such a patient?

There are some perennial favorites. Paranoid delusions are always fun for an analyst, but try to keep up with the latest technology. Microwaves programmed by Martians to emit death rays are old hat. Many patients complain of their home computers exerting mind control. *Notice that all really good paranoid delusions have a germ of truth.*

Like everything else, analysis goes through fads. Madonna is credited with the recent surge of interest in narcissism. Treating agoraphobics was modish for a while, but when analysts realized that these people missed almost all their appointments, they lost interest. Eating disorders enjoyed a brief binge until analysts got tired of picking crumbs off the couch and grew embarrassed about bumping into their patients at Weight Watchers. Stressed-out investment bankers were desirable before Black Monday, 1987, then went into a decline, and are now on the upswing again (unless they're subjects of an SEC probe). Split personalities began to proliferate when Vickie was given two lives to live on *One Life to Live*. If you have the presence of mind to remember that there's always a good self and a bad self, your analyst will immediately realize that he is working with a higher-level neurotic.

Sexual dysfunction and fetishism are always interesting, but are getting harder and harder to find. Think reptiles. A little inventiveness sometimes helps. Suppose you're a man whose issue is that casual sexual relationships with several women does not gratify a need for companionship but you are deathly afraid of committing yourself. If you share a little shaft of insight from the writer Alfred Polgar, "Many are too little, one is too much," then at least you offer the analyst some small hope that there are decent prospects out there for his women patients.

Unwritten Rules for Bringing the Session to a Close

By now, it is common knowledge that every analyst has watches on each wrist and clocks tactfully hidden throughout his office so that there is absolutely no chance at all that the session will run even one minute over. This is a by-product of Freud's unhappy experience with obsessional patients in his pioneering days back in Vienna. These cruel, exploitative characters would take advantage of the fact that Freud was a gentleman. They would seize on any opportunity, fair or foul, to prolong the session. No sooner would Freud begin to rise from behind the couch than they would go into high gear with an endless stream of subordinate and qualifying phrases. While Freud stood helplessly by, trying to observe the normal rules of politeness, the patient (whose mother's milk was undoubtedly sour) would say, "Let me tell you just one short dream before I leave." It is no wonder, then, that Freud confided to his good friend Tyler, "If I kill one of my patients, do you think it would affect the transference for the others?"

Today's analysts are made of much sterner stuff. American neurotics wouldn't dare say, "Just one more thing..." The unwritten rule of analysis is: Respect the analyst's timetable. It would be a serious mistake, indeed, to think that everything is arranged to serve your interests exclusively.

With this in mind, we now turn to one of the niftiest gambits of the successful neurotic, the game of "Find the Analyst's Clock." The typical analyst has clocks planted all over the place so that he can sneak surreptitious glances at the time. This tactic is particularly noticeable during the early sessions, when the analyst must sneak a peek while sitting face to face.

Constantly needing to know the time puts the analyst in a terrible bind. If you catch him looking at the clock, you will hurt and humiliate him. Analysts who have been caught in the act have been called uncaring, mercenary, calculating, insincere, detached, and exploitative. On the other hand, the analyst must know the time so as not to make you feel dismissed in mid-sentence and to be considerate of the next patient's appointment.

SICR advises its clients to catch the analyst's eye so that he knows perfectly well that you know the game. At the same time, in the gentlest way possible, smile reassuringly and let him down ever so gently. De-escalate the session on your own—bring up no crises in the last ten minutes, never toss in controversial material ("Oh, by the way...") and if you're really up to it, ask if it would be all right if you left a little early: you have to meet a friend at Bloomingdale's

Even to the most dedicated analyst, time is money. The intelligent neurotic should share this heavy responsibility by taking the hint and ending the session without having to be asked. The average analyst has 4.5 clocks scattered throughout his office to heighten the patient's awareness.

Questions You Should Never Ask

One of the legacies of the classical analyst is a reluctance to answer questions or give advice. The real reasons for this reserve are (a) the analyst has a paranoid fear that behind every question is a trap and (b) he does not have any neutral answers or good advice. In typical response to hazardous questioning the analyst retreats into total silence and calls himself "Freudian." Consider the following three questions:

1. Can I call you at home?
2. Where are you going on vacation?
3. Where did you get your training?

All are seemingly innocent questions yet each one is insidious. The best way to allay the analyst's fears is to learn to distinguish between safe and provocative questions. Obviously, "Were you married once before?" is intrusive. So is, "Do you have any children?"—the veiled implication is that the analyst might not have children or might have the wrong kind of children or that the analyst might not know the first thing about bringing up children.

The psychoanalyst Hyman Spotnitz described the following incident: "One day, a patient whom I had been treating for a long time picked up a massive ashtray and hurled it in my direction. It missed my head by just a few inches. When I asked her how she happened to miss, she said, 'I still like you.'"

What Spotnitz neglected to say is that in the third year of training, every psychoanalyst learns how to duck. Some patients, however, have a wonderful knack for getting to their analyst no matter how skilled he is at ducking. Their questions, which often conceal more than they reveal, make the analyst tense and on edge, understandably cautious and fearful that he is being led into a trap.

When SICR polled its membership for the type of questions that patients should think twice about asking, the following questions led the list. Invariably, they were raised by passive-aggressive, immature individuals like you who are object-lessons in masochism. For once, see if you can control your repressed hostility. Limit yourself to one, or at most two, of these questions during any given session and then lie low for a week or two:

- Can I leave my dog in the waiting room?
- Do you think about me between sessions?
- How long will this treatment take?
- Do you mind if I put this coffee down here? Whoops!
- Can someone like me be cured?
- Do you have any aspirins?
- Could you talk more?
- Who does your decorating?
- Have you ever treated anyone like me?

- Would you call my wife and tell her I'm not angry with her anymore?
- Were you ever divorced?
- Do you live here?
- Why can't I get over my troubles by myself?
- If I change my external life situation, won't my problems be cured?
- How can there be an unconscious?
- What should I do if I don't dream?
- What's the *real* cause of my problems?
- How can emotional problems start in childhood?
- I know my personality has not been what it should be, but how could this cause my problems?
- Am I different than other people? (Absolutely the worst of all possible questions; leaves you wide open for the real truth.)
- Aren't there any shortcuts?
- I heard that people are supposed to fall in love with their analysts; what should I do if I don't feel that way about you?
- I still can't believe that talking is going to be enough for me to get better. Will it?
- My friend's analyst doesn't charge for missed appointments and cancellations. Do you?
- Oh, by the way, I'm taking a three-week vacation in July. When do you take yours?

Jokes—They're Not Funny

Analysis is not the place for a patient to tell jokes. Those who feel compelled to ask, "Did you hear the one about...?" will be seen as someone who mistakes the session for a meeting of the Elks Club. This is serious business, not a place for cocktail party chitchat or hail-fellow-well-met camaraderie.

On the other hand, an analyst tells a joke for an entirely different purpose. He's trying to make you receptive to a new or difficult point. He figures if he gets you to laugh, you'll be more open: Be sure to laugh at the punchline, but don't forget

Your Own Worst Enemy

Joyce Cary once said, "It is a tragedy of the world that no one knows what he doesn't know, and the less a man knows the more sure he is that he knows everything." This is my very polite way of saying that neurotics like you are your own worst enemy. Your constant manipulations and attempts at one-upsmanship, your devious minds in search of the "good breast" you never deserved, the transparent ploys you insist on recycling—will only make your analyst mumble to himself, "Strike one."

SICR has polled its members for the figures of speech universally agreed upon as glaring patient blunders. Test out your neurotic unconscious. See if you can pick up what's wrong with each of these statements:

- Do you remember how we ended our last session?
- I would be more than happy...
- Incidentally...
- To be honest...
- To tell the truth...
- Before I forget...
- You see what I mean?...
- I don't want to upset you but...
- It's none of my business but...
- It goes without saying...
- I was just kidding...
- Hiya Stranger!
- Don't worry...
- Just one more thing...
- I already told you this, but...
- I have one or two *idiosyncracies*

the reason you're on the couch. For some reason, analysts love to explain by using obscure similies, metaphors, analogies, and figures of speech. They prefer to believe that they're dealing with intelligent neurotics.

Consider the following examples of analytic humor and see if you can guess the theme the analyst is driving at.

Joke 1: A loser asked his friend, who was very successful in seducing women, how to do it. "Easy," the swinger said. "Make a date. Then a few hours before the date, call the chick and tell her you're unbelievably pooped, can't go out, but that if she wouldn't mind coming over, you'll whip up a dinner and you can spend a quiet evening. She'll probably say yes, so you can get a big steak, a fine wine, prepare soft lights and romantic music. She'll help you with the dishes and it will feel very intimate and domestic. You ask her to dance, dance her into the bedroom, put her down on the bed, and you're in!"

Meeting his constricted friend a week later, the swinger asked him if he'd tried it. "Yes." "Did it work?" "No." "What happened?" "Well, I called her like you suggested and she came over. Steak, wine, soft lights, and romantic music. We washed the dishes. Then we danced close. I danced her into the bedroom, I pushed her onto the bed, and we got undressed." "So?" "So, just as I was putting my shoe trees into my shoes, she got up and left."

(This joke is specially designed for you infuriating compulsives out there who lose the forest for the trees. If the analyst resorts to this old clinker, it's a sure sign that he's getting impatient.)

Joke 2: Said the five-year-old to the four-year-old as they peeked through the keyhole of their parents' bedroom: "And they yell at us for picking our noses!" (The analyst is trying to shock you into talking for real. He sees you as squeamish and square and wants to test out your unconscious to see if it has any elasticity.)

Joke 3: A man meets an old friend who asks him for a hundred dollars. He answers, "Sorry, I don't have it." First man: "Then how about fifty?" Second man: "Don't have that either." First: "Twenty?" Second: "No." First: "Five?" Second: "Sorry." First: "A dollar?" Second: "Can't spare it." First: "A dime?" Second: "No." First (desperately): "Then how about carrying me!" (Good for patients who refuse to grow up.)

Joke 4: One evening after dark, a young couple were taking a pleasant walk along a city street bordering some woods. They came upon a man crawling around on hands and knees under a streetlight. They stopped, said, "Good evening," while the man continued searching in the grass. They asked what he had lost, and he said that it was a silver dollar. They asked, "Where do you think you lost it?" He answered, "Oh, it was over in the woods." "So why are you looking here?" they said. "There's no use looking in the dark." (For patients who are afraid to examine the scary stuff inside.)

My wife and I realized that all the plants in our house were dying. We tried to discover the cause, but we'd just about given up and were very disturbed because we love our plants. One day we saw the maid pouring what seemed like a very unnecessary amount of water into each one of the plants. Then we realized what the problem was. The plants were being drowned. We told the maid to please put less water in, but we kept noticing her sneaking around and continuing to put water in despite our reminder. Finally, out of desperation, we severely rebuked her and told her, please, no more water. An hour later my wife came into the living room and found the maid secretly pouring water into one of the larger plants, which had cost over a thousand dollars and was on its last legs. My wife said, "I can't believe you're doing this. What is the matter with you?" The maid looked up at her beseechingly, the pitcher of water in her hand, and said with a motion toward the plant, "Just a little?" (This anecdote is used as a reminder that compulsions have nothing to do with reality.)

If you don't get the point, laugh anyway; then go home and ask your friend to ask his analyst what it means. SICR now publishes a handy reference guide, *Obscure Citations*. This convenient volume is a collection of "insider jokes" that analysts repeatedly use even though their meanings are generally obscure.

Here, I'll try an easy one on you to see whether you're catching on yet.

A man was grumbling day after day about the contents of his sandwiches. When his colleagues had heard enough, they suggested that he ask his wife to make something different. The worker retorted, "Wife? I make those sandwiches myself."

Doing Right By Doing Good

Some perfectly deserving patients lose valuable opportunities to win over their analyst by letting jealousy get in the way. Even though these patients think their analysts are wonderful, they would never think of referring a friend or colleague to him because they are incapable of sharing a good thing. Patients who can overcome this immature emotion should concentrate on referring patients by the droves to make the analyst feel happy and appreciated.

All you have to do is keep your eye out for likely candidates. Whether you are in an office, library, classroom, airplane, or at a ball game, there are always people who are in distress and have something missing from their lives. A little effort to draw someone out at the right time can do wonders. One patient was in his dentist's chair right before his analytic hour. He asked the dentist if everything was all right because he looked upset. The dentist, who was visibly moved by such a kind gesture, said, "Do you know what it's like to be fifty-five and not be able to get it up?" The dentist proceeded to put down his tools and pour out all of his feelings with the patient, who then took the dentist by the hand, led him to his analyst, and gave the dentist his hour.

Another patient, by running around and lending a sympathetic ear at the right time, was able to deliver everyone in Section 17 of Giants Stadium to his analyst's office. Always carry your analyst's business cards with you and be on the alert for people who cry at comedies, talk back to bank ATM machines, and carry their own silverware to restaurants.

The patient who is alert to these possibilities in daily life is practicing compassion, empathy, and all the other caring emotions that will make his analyst proud of him. When you start receiving birthday cards from your analyst, it's a sign that you're getting the hang of things.

Practical Details

It is important to straighten out practical matters, in the beginning to avoid potential misunderstandings. Be sure to discuss the number of sessions per week, the length of each session, the question of fixed or varying hours of attendance, the number and duration of holiday breaks, fees, method and time of payment, the problem of canceled sessions, and the preferred mode of emergency communication between analyst and patient. In every one of these matters, try to sense what would meet the analyst's requirements and act accordingly. He has to go through this petty nonsense with every new patient so try to remember that in most cases you're only one person.

Though you may think you're acting appreciative and friendly during the discussion of this dull, dry material, that may not be enough. The analyst might need something that goes beyond friendly—how about standing up just once and saying, "Bravo, I think you've covered everything!"

When the analysts says, "All right already, let's get down to business," you know you've gotten to first base. The list of practical details should include:

• *Kleptomania in the Waiting Room.* Stealing other people's umbrellas requires only an interpretation; "borrowing" the analyst's magazines, however, is a much more serious offense, often punishable by discharge.

• *Number of Sessions.* If the analyst looks overworked, see him once a week and talk to your wife or husband the rest of the time. If he looks like he could use a new suit, leave it to his discretion.

• *Length of session.* When the analyst tells you the sessions generally run fifty minutes, be generous. Tell him, "Live a little. All my friends' analysts only give them forty-five minutes. That's all I expect."

• *Attendance.* When it comes time to agree on the hours of the sessions, some patients can be very selfish and demanding. Be a mensch.* Make yourself available at *his* convenience.

• *Holiday Breaks.* Ask the analyst for an official analytic holiday calendar which includes all state and national observances, and, of course, Sigmund Freud's birthday. Analysts understandably charge for all holiday and vacation breaks; after all, they deserve a paid vacation, don't they?

• *Payment.* In this area particularly, don't be a schnorrer or a compulsive bargainer.† You get exactly what you pay for. Don't let pettiness be your downfall. Or as Freud put it, "If you want to drown yourself, don't do it in shallow water."

An affluent lady from Great Neck had all kinds of friends going to analysis. When the analyst announced his fee, she blinked three times but didn't say anything. The next session she came in and said, "I don't understand it. None of my friends pay that kind of fee. You're not even an M.D., it's an extremely high fee. They never heard of such a thing, and by the way, what is your range?" "One hundred, two hundred dollars." "Two hundred dollars? Who pays two hundred?" "Nobody, but you asked me what my range is."

Charlie Brown's therapist, Lucy, charged only five cents, but she didn't work in the high-rent district. Woody Allen has commented that he and his analyst disagreed vehemently on how he should claim the money he spent for analysis on his tax

---

*A decent person; someone of admirable character.
†A chisler; one with an instinct for exploiting and assuaging guilt in the analyst.

returns. The analyst insisted that the costs should be listed under medical expenses, but Woody felt that entertainment would be most suitable. They finally compromised and listed the analysis under religious contributions.

With regard to the matter of fees, the analyst has anything but a holier-than-thou attitude. The fact is, he feels distinctly uncomfortable with even the slightest hint that he chose psychoanalysis as a profession because it affords him a good living. The matter of feees (Freudian slip) is an awkward topic but must be frankly discussed in the very first session, and you are the one who may have to bring it up. The analyst finds it much easier to broach the most intimate matters than to speak of filthy, dirty lucre.*

Do not be so boorish as to ask, "How much is this going to cost?" How can a price be placed on your emotional well-being? Was anyone in your life ever willing to listen to you for a solid hour for even a million dollars?

The easiest way to handle the matter of fees is to simply hand over your last three W-2 forms, admit to all the money you've siphoned off, and wait for a number. Analyst's fees typically range from about $75 to $200 per hour and up. The higher fees are usually set by "star" analysts who have their own TV shows, have successfully rid entire heavy-metal rock groups of drug dependencies, or have books on the bestseller lists (see map). The $75 hourly fee was reportedly charged once by an analyst in Dubuque for a patient who was a single mother of five on welfare awaiting a kidney transplant donor.

Cancelled Sessions. You don't need a reason to be absent. Just be sure to pay and it'll be the basis for a friendly discussion. The analyst will no doubt be hurt anyway and will most probably take it personally, but as long as you know that

---

*This is because Freud equated money with feces but forgot exactly why. Nevertheless, this has established the custom of never paying the analyst directly, but always placing the check on his desk instead.

Fee Structure

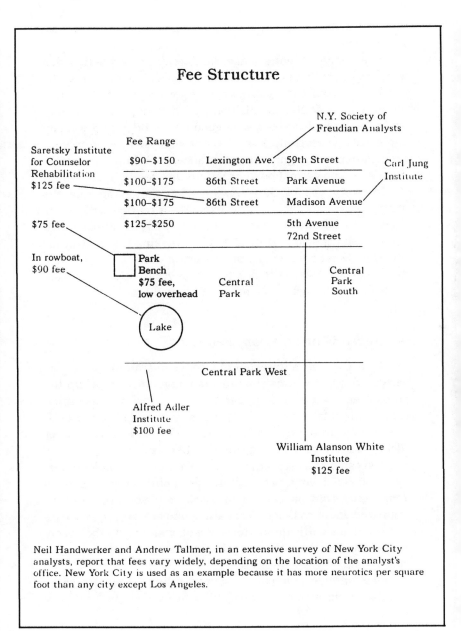

N.Y. Society of
Freudian Analysts

Saretsky Institute   Fee Range
for Counselor $90–$150   Lexington Ave.   59th Street
Rehabilitation   Carl Jung
$125 fee $100–$175   86th Street   Park Avenue   Institute

                      $100–$175   86th Street   Madison Avenue

$75 fee $125–$250   5th Avenue
                                                        72nd Street

In rowboat,
$90 fee   **Park**
                         Bench
                         $75 fee,   Central   Central
                         low overhead   Park   Park
                                                                South

                         Lake

                         Central Park West

                   Alfred Adler
                   Institute
                   $100 fee

                                        William Alanson White
                                              Institute
                                              $125 fee

Neil Handwerker and Andrew Tallmer, in an extensive survey of New York City
analysts, report that fees vary widely, depending on the location of the analyst's
office. New York City is used as an example because it has more neurotics per square
foot than any city except Los Angeles.

you're responsible for each and every session, he'll try to be a sport about it.

The analyst is not a judge; he doesn't know whether you were right or wrong for not coming. He appreciates the courtesy of your letting him know if you're going to be thirty minutes late. Still and all, don't push your luck. Marshall McLuhan provided you with a good out—"I don't necessarily agree with everything I say." If the analyst interprets your cancellation as a significant resistance, give him your attention. Who knows, maybe your wife didn't really have twins.

In every one of these matters, keep in mind that the analyst has to go through this exhausting routine with every single new patient. unless you're absolutely convinced that you're a split personality, start off by making this part of his life easy. Don't get hung up on irrelevant details. (By the way, most analysts' favorite Ben & Jerry's flavor is either Chocolate Chip Cookie Dough or Rain Forest Crunch.)

Advanced Waiting Room Behavior

At SICR, we advise our neurotics-in-training to arrive early and use the extra time to good advantage. Fluff up the pillows, empty the wastepaper basket, restock the magazine rack, bring fresh flowers. Keep your eyes peeled. Don't hesitate to turn in anybody who changes the station, smokes, or filches magazines. Nothing succeeds like excess.

You can also use this time to psych out the few patients who have survived your early strategies. Polish off the Sunday *Times* crossword puzzle in pen. Look as if you are into self-improvement or consciousness-raising and are here to take care of a small, insignificant matter while on your way to the beach. Subtly make the others feel increasingly self-conscious, clumsy, and slightly unpleasant.

One unforgettable patient spent her lunch hours for years circulating through every analyst's waiting room in New York

City and its suburbs, discreetly passing out her analyst's calling card and raving about how terrific he was. As the other patients deserted their own analysts in droves and flocked to Dr. X, he started receiving complaints from his colleagues. At the next session, Dr. X told his patient about the problem she had created and gently chided her. But the patient, a brilliant neurotic if ever there was one, noticed that he winked.

CHAPTER V

What Your Analyst Does to Himself for You

Stuck inside these four walls.
Sent inside forever.
Never meeting no one nice again.

PAUL & LINDA MC CARTNEY

Man does not live by reality alone. An analyst's prolonged exposure to his patients does terrible things to his capacity to experience the joys and sorrows that ordinary people feel. Analysts tend to gradually lose their own personal identities. One analyst actually broke down when he realized he was working on a lovely Memorial Day while a patient was taking his children to the big parade. Treasured memories of being with his father floated past. The guns, the tanks, the bayonets, the rifles, and the machine guns. The patient tried to coax the analyst not to be such a stick-in-the-mud, to give himself a break. "Come on along. The children won't mind. I'll tell them you're my uncle. And then we'll go to the zoo and I'll buy you some popcorn and you can feed the animals." The analyst's resolve broke down—he canceled his last six patients. The last I heard, he was working in a bikini as a consulting psychologist for Club Med in Tahiti.

The average analyst is an anachronism. He works in splendid isolation, has no executive associates, possesses no fax machine, doesn't know how to use a computer, and is rarely hip or stylish. He has a gift for listening and understanding, but the price he must pay for his objectivity is emotional celibacy. In sitting and listening, he renounces man's basic instinct to talk.

The analyst is sworn to be anonymous, nondescript, a mirror. If he has needs at all, they must never be brought to the patient's awareness. No Freudian analyst in human memory has ever gone to the bathroom, called his stockbroker, or taken a coffee break during a session.

The Little Professor

What were the rewards that led him to this trying profession? It has been shown that the average analyst needs to be needed. He enjoys the vicarious satisfaction of being deeply involved in people's lives and likes nothing more than the feeling that he's being helpful and is appreciated.

Studies have shown that the typical analyst was, as a child, often the family therapist, wise beyond his years. Instead of playing in the schoolyard, he rushed home to keep his mother company so that she wouldn't become just another forgotten latchkey mother. He refereed his parents' fights, minded his kid sisters without complaining, and never asked for an allowance. Parents of the precocious tot often misused him and rushed him through childhood. Understanding too much too soon, the analyst-in-the-making had to forgo the normal pleasures of being a juvenile delinquent, owning a black leather jacket and feeling up girls at the movies.

By their adult years, analysts are supposed to be bastions of strength and wisdom. They have been trained to expect no gratitude, to discourage even the smallest gift, to apologize for vacations, and to control every impulse to grow closer to other humans. They unconsciously hope to fill their insatiable need for love and attention, never daring to admit openly that they have any real needs of their own.

The strain of continuously being in a role—wise, concerned, and deeply involved but never distracted or provoked—is often too much for an analyst to handle. Looking away embarrassedly while a liberated patient nurses her baby during the session, or fighting a losing battle to prevent his wife from redecorating the office, is often far more draining than dealing with the most complicated neurosis. Nevertheless, the vast majority of analysts are sturdy, honest, decent people who mean well and who, in their own way, really make a difference.

Katz, in his twisted masterpiece *What Is a Phallus?* reminds us, however, that the abnormal restraint required in working with sexy streamlined neurosis cannot help but take a terrible toll on the human mind. On the other hand, M. Chasen reminds us that even devoting an entire lifetime to a benign topic like the foot fetish is no guarantee of mental stability. In the much-cited *Joy of Sox* he makes a strong case that wearing socks to bed is the secret to having multiple orgasms. And what are we to make of R. Levine, burned out at thirty-eight, who spent nearly ten years before his breakdown completing *From Food to Fertilizer: The Role of Excrement in Our Daily Lives*. His most memorable line still lives with us: "We all sit on a pile of shit complaining of the smell." His favorite TV program was *Social Security in Action*.

In *A Fine Mind Gone Mad*, Haley, Brya, and Goldberg (1983) warn us that an analyst's shingle is no guarantee that he is not nitwitted. There are some real weirdos out there. Behind all the psychobabble and the trappings of pseudo-scientific trendiness, you could be in the hands of a demented analyst who uses only the wrong side of his brain.

A patient who had insomnia recently came to me for a second opinion. His first analyst had reassuringly advised him not to lose any sleep over it.

For only $10 a month, you can subscribe to the SICR hotline, which has recorded announcements that name the names of analysts to steer clear of. What follows are profiles of brain-dead analysts. Judge for yourself.

The Obsessive-Compulsive Analyst. This nervous type is wracked by many doubts and uncertainties. He has yet to see a problem, however complicated, which, when examined closely, did not become still more complicated.

He regards you as a puzzlement, a frustration, the cause of many sleepless nights. He puts you on the couch, takes you off the couch, tries the phallic mother interpretation, the castrating father approach; nothing seems to work. Some patients even have described the unnerving experience of having this analyst leap from his chair in the middle of a session, pull feverishly at yellowed journals on the shelves, and pore through the contents before shouting a victorious, "Aha!"

This analyst's reputation for cool detachment and laboratory manner obviously is a myth. Most people don't realize that privately he's a nervous wreck. He takes the whole thing too seriously.

His instinct is to keep babbling until he sees the light. But you can rest easy. He will finally find a neurosis worthy of your personality. The secret here is to avoid changing your mind about what's the matter. That will confuse him unnecessarily. If you just have patience, he will discover something nice and interesting for the two of you to work on until he goes to his next seminar.

As Montaigne once observed, "No one is exempt from talking nonsense. The misfortune is to do it solemnly." The overtly obsessive analyst has all the charm of an alienist probing the true identity of Santa Claus. Get out while the going is good.

The Masochistic Analyst. Here is a man who derives unconscious gratification from the anxiety he arouses in his patients and the difficulties he creates for himself. He has a reputation for being good with difficult cases, thereby developing a practice almost exclusively devoted to other analysts' castoffs.

The masochist charges too little and waits for the patient to feel guilty enough to voluntarily raise his fee. This sounds good until you start wondering if he isn't charging others even less.

His sessions frequently run overtime, and the waiting patient becomes annoyed. In this way, he acts out the self-fulfilling prophecy of doing good at his own expense.

The Voyeuristic Analyst. All analysts suffer from this malady to one extent or another. A couch, a desk, and a notepad are his only protection against accusations of being a "peeping Tom." He tries to appear as if nothing you can say will shock him. He dreams of having Marla and Donald call him up for marriage counseling and would love to be in Dr. Ruth's shoes so he could hear all about "what people do with the animals."

The Infallible Analyst. The infallible analyst enjoys the sound of his own voice clapping. He has an overblown ego that he constantly trips over. He believes he cannot be fooled, misled, or confused and will never admit to being wrong.

His interpretations are broad and oversimplified but ooze hearty optimism, as in: "So you were fired again? How will that matter in the long run?"

The infallible analyst feels the patient can be magically healed through the strength of his convictions alone. So taken is he with his own brilliance that he often loses sight of whether or not his interpretations have any relevance to what's really bothering the patient.

His charisma is, however, very persuasive. Because he is prone to writing many self-serving books and articles, the patient may benefit greatly by just reading about himself as a miraculous cure.

Patient Envy. By far the most common ailment of analysts of all types is patient envy. Analysts constantly imagine that their colleagues have better practices.

Women are much more likely to undergo analysis, which has resulted in good male patients being in such demand that many analysts feel inferior if they don't have a significant number of males in treatment. This has led to a vast underground economy in which analysts constantly trade patients with one another. The going rate in January 1989 was two single, middle-aged women for every homophobic, repressed man. Analysts also like to treat a nice, representative cross-section of the most common current neuroses. Narcissists are all the rage now. Borderline personalities—though always a puzzlement—are highly desirable.

One schizophrenic is worth three hysterics, and an ordinary depressive is worth absolutely nothing unless there's some manic with it.

If your analyst suggests that he is transferring you to somebody else, there is no reason to blame yourself. It is considered perfectly good form, however, to ask the reason for the recommendation, who you have been traded for, and whether you're being sent down to the minors.

Letting Your Analyst Have a Life— Why Should You?

Your analyst is well acquainted with the weariness, fever, fret of existence; he has a whole other life outside the consulting room. This is a reality not easily grasped, but if you come to accept it, the analyst himself may someday believe it.

For the patient who wishes to be the analyst's darling, a better understanding of the analyst's "other" life is necessary. Put yourself in his place and try to understand the trials and tribulations of his daily struggle just to get by.

Your capacity to become an A+ patient depends on your ability to forego your own problems and consider the everyday reality of your analyst's life. How else will he know if you can be trusted? Acting in your interest, your analyst will provide you with trials and test cases to see whether you can react appropriately to common life situations.

- You find yourself in a hot tub with your analyst.
- You see your analyst seated in front of you in an assertiveness training group.
- You come to a meeting of Weight Watchers Anonymous and hear your analyst confessing how he's "cheated" during the week.
- You spot your analyst in a dark romantic corner of a restaurant with a woman who is obviously not his wife.
- Your analyst is inadvertently seated at your table at a wedding.
- You see your analyst trying on a bathing suit in the communal dressing room at Loehmann's.
- Your analyst is enrolled in the same adult education course as you—Fly Without Fear.
- You hear some choice gossip about your analyst. Should you or shouldn't you tell him?

The Analyst's Family

For many patients, the first hint that their analyst has a family comes when they call him at home one evening and hear someone shrieking in the background, "What do they want from your life?" This is the analyst's spouse, who is convinced that all the patients get more time and consideration than she does.

Considering the spouse's attitude, it is best never to make the mistake, if you leave a message with her on the phone, of sounding attractive, exciting, or interesting. "I'm just another dull, draining neurotic" is the best image to project.

Despite knowing that most of the people in her husband's practice are quite neurotic, the wife can never understand how it is possible for so many of them to idolize him. The analyst retaliates (unconsciously of course) by trying to drive her insane with little stories of how fascinating and attractive his female patients are and how yet another one tried to seduce him.

If you are a female seeing a female analyst, and her

husband answers the phone when you call her at home, pretend to be selling magazine subscriptions. He is probably a chauvinist who secretly resents anything that cuts into his precious time, and is convinced he is doing his wife a favor by letting her work fifty hours a week.

If you are a male and your analyst's husband answers the phone, hang up. If you don't, she is going to have to spend the entire night defensively persuading him that you're not having an affair with her, that you have a low libido and a small penis besides; and then she won't have any good interpretations left for you.

The Home Office

If a man's home is his hassle, then the analyst who maintains an office in his home will feel particularly exposed and vulnerable, because many aspects of his anonymity will be spoiled through events entirely out of his control.

The patient may discover that his analyst is always the butt of the household's inside jokes. Do not take it seriously if the maid announces, "The anal retentive is on the phone."

Members of the family may mimic the "doctor's" voice he assumes when a patient calls. They may put you on hold and play "Name That Psycho." If you catch one of his teenage children, you may even be told that he is calm and understanding with patients but a raving lunatic on the subject of car keys.

The analyst with a home office is continually self-conscious about what his patients see and hear. He must ask for a fee increase knowing that you've noticed the new Jaguar in the driveway with the license plate "Born to Shop." He wrestles with the question of what to do about the fact that he can't hear you because his son is playing "Live Like a Suicide" at top volume on the floor above the office. Should he ignore it or go upstairs, drop his decorum, and scream bloody murder? The analyst's dog is not even allowed to bark.

If you are going to see an analyst with a home office, it is wise to choose one whose house costs roughly the same as your own. If you're on a four-acre estate and he's got a 50 x 100 plot, your secret superiority, smugness, and patronizing tone will surely creep out in your dreams and humiliate him.

On the other hand, if you've got a five-room split and he's in a three-story colonial with stable and carriage house, your jealousy, hostility, and competitiveness will so pervade the sessions that the poor analyst will be unable to enjoy his good fortune.

Unconsciously, many patients with less luxurious homes than their analyst's pay late because they assume the analyst doesn't need the money. This is a neurotic reaction which fails to take into account the analyst's wife's wanton shopping habits and the fact that he has to work Saturdays to pay for the gardener.

Weekends, Holidays, and August

Analysts are notorious for suffering from feelings of desertion and abandonment. Before you leave for a long vacation, reassure him that you will definitely return and promise to see him for an extra session or two as soon as you get back.

Many analysts suffer from "Sunday Depression" and "August Angst"—a marked feeling of unreality which stems from being face-to-face with a wife who claims he never talks to her, and three crabby kids. He even begins to fantasize about his telephone ringing with a call from a patient with a nice, solvable problem.

During vacations, patients should send cheery postcards, support the analyst's need for rest and recuperation, and develop many crises that they just manage to get through. They should return in September with acute separation dreams and enough issues to carry over treatment till the following July.

Emergencies

Before your analyst leaves for vacation, he will provide you with the name of another analyst in case of an emergency.

What he is doing is compensating for his guilt about leaving his patients by pretending to have the humility to believe someone else could replace him. Nobody ever takes the analyst up on his offer of a replacement, and he doesn't really mean it. Besides, what kind of analyst works in August? Your analyst knows that is how you feel and feels safe offering you a name.

If you must call the substitute analyst, keep in mind that your own analyst will be narcissistically wounded and will seriously question the hostile motives behind your action. Cover yourself by asking him his policies about phone sessions before he goes.

CHAPTER VI

Helping Your Analyst to Survive Everything

The world is flat, stale and unprofitable...

HAMLET

Not surprisingly, most analysts are privately repelled by the fads and fashions of the "me" generation and the age of "healthy" narcissism. How do you tell a fanatic born-again vegetarian not to take himself so seriously (or gently break the news that there's nothing like a good thick steak)? The fitness craze has now become so absurd that many analysts have signs in their waiting rooms that say, "Please do not engage in low-impact aerobics while free-associating."

Most analysts believe that the New Age neuroses are nothing but a study of trivial pursuits. They're impatient with the fast-track neurotics who think life is one self-actualization after another. And what analyst can help but be less than overwhelmed by one of those codependent women who love too much and make foolish choices about men who hate them?

Narcissistic Chutzpah*

The contemporary analyst looks back with nostalgia on the simple pleasures of the Golden Age of Psychoanalysis. Freud

---

*Narcissistic *chutzpah* was a concept first introduced by Bryce & Haley. The precise definition is very elusive, but it has something to do with the fact that certain clinical types possess incredible gall. The classic illustration is the youth who murders his parents and pleads to the court for mercy on the grounds that he is an orphan.

"Oedipus doesn't aggravate *his* mother like this."

kept himself in shape warding off the amorous advances of beautiful, seductive hysterics who would suddenly leap off the couch and breathlessly insist that the love and passion they felt for him was real. Being chased around the office while tossing brilliant interpretations over one's shoulder at least creates an air of spontaneity and erotic excitement, compared to the sterile rewards involved in treating patients in the 1990s, who negotiate fees while reminding the analyst that "this is a buyer's market," and who pride themselves on marching on Penis Awareness Day.

Like that movie with Dudley Moore and Elizabeth McGovern, where Moore plays an analyst who feels harried and overwhelmed by his busy practice. Freud and Jung visit to see him in a dream and Freud says, "I'm sorry; I never meant to create such an industry."

Modern technology has even invaded that old standby, the unconscious. How does one remain unperturbed by a patient who asks if he can fax his dreams so the analyst can think about them between sessions? And what would *you* feel if a patient, Type A or not, asked if he could have his sessions by cellular phone because he wants to beat the traffic home? Today's analyst must appear unruffled when the patient quotes Dr. Ruth as the final authority on sex and insists that the analyst listen to her program so he won't be so confused next time about the exact distinction between clitoral and vaginal orgasms, or the scientific fact that men have G spots and suffer from postpartum depressions. In the face of these brazen assaults, the vaunted neutrality and scientific detachment of most analysts' psyches has begun to more closely resemble a stroll through Stephen King's backyard.

The Bad Analyst Feeling: The Course, Its Onset; the Recovery, and Its Aftermath

The Schlappschwanz Syndrome was first notice by Freud in 1906 in *The Illness That Has No Name*. In this early classic, Freud describes a paranoid night when he came home to dinner after a particularly grueling day. Against his will, he found himself criticizing his beloved wife Martha's cooking efforts by voicing suspicions about why the matzoh balls insisted on sinking to the bottom of the bowl. In his autobiography, he remembers telling his confidante, L. Epstein, "He who, like us, unearths the most wicked dreams that he might fight them, must be prepared to suffer damage himself in this contest."

Beginning in 1987 and continuing to the present, a mental disorder of epidemic proportions has begun to surface in the analytic population. Over 80 percent of the analysts who consulted SICR during this period reported strange feelings of agoraphobia. The symptoms are typically unrecognized, mis-diagnosed, or improperly treated.

The agoraphobic analyst is best described as having a morbid fear of empty waiting rooms and open hours. In the throes of this terrifying syndrome, he is afraid to leave the security of his own home for the office. He typically avoids entering into any situation from which there is no easy escape route. What does the dedicated analyst do, for example, if he still has four patient-hours left but the phone hasn't rung once this week with a new referral? No matter how primitive his abandonment fears, he can't simply give in to his panic and leave the remaining patients in the lurch.

The onset of this disorder is characterized by unrealistic worrying, a feeling of not being useful or needed, smothering sensations, hot or cold flashes, the fear of going crazy, and in its most serious form, a premonition that August is going to be a terrible month and that maybe he should start taking off right after Memorial Day.

Though evidence on the question remains quite mixed, the general consensus is that a hypersensitivity to early separation experiences seems to be the core problem. Analysts who suspect that their parents deliberately left them behind at the beach when they were young, or sent them to sleep-away camps in infancy during the pre-oedipal period are par-ticularly susceptible.

In a recovery group, one analyst dredged up a markedly

upsetting memory. While away in a supposedly nonsectarian camp, he nevertheless found himself waiting in a confessional line during Sunday services. Being Jewish and unfamiliar with the ritual, the analyst (as a child) turned to his friend standing next to him and asked what he should do. The kid said, "He smiles if you tell him you masturbate a lot." When the analyst mentioned that he didn't know what masturbation was, the kid said, "It doesn't matter. He still smiles." Then the analyst (as an adult) remembered wanting to overcome his fears and loneliness by assimilating with the other boys in the bunk. He began to hear rumors that this "Pope" guy was pretty important, so he went around bragging for a week that his father knew the Pope personally and played pinochle with him every Saturday night.

The Vulnerable Analyst; or,
The Patient Is the Enemy

Old Sigmund knew what he was talking about. When an analyst is in a vulnerable mental state, he should not be left unattended. He needs a little companionship, a human touch, a bit of humor perhaps—a lifeline to sanity. In the grip of a grimly serious approach to life, it is easy for an analyst to imagine that the patients in the waiting room are comparing notes and conspiring to leave him en masse. He looks forward to a meaty Freudian slip or a patient who leaves his umbrella behind. But nothing seems to go right. He feels hurt and depressed when no one has reported erotic dreams or romantic fantasies to him in over a week, and he begins to wonder why his colleagues all have sexier practices.

UFOs and Your Analyst

As if psychoanalysts didn't have enough to contend with, the latest craze to hit the psychoanalytic community is the UFO neurosis. An increasing number of otherwise ordinary patients report that they were late for their sessions because they were kidnapped by aliens right off the streets in broad daylight in midtown Manhattan. Many analysts are becoming jittery that now they are in on the secret, they may be next.

THE UFO ABDUCTION SYNDROME

A REPORT ON STRANGE AND UNUSUAL EXPERIENCES ASSOCIATED WITH UFO ABDUCTIONS BASED UPON SICR'S SURVEY OF 20,911 AMERICAN ADULTS

**R. Mendelsohn, Ph.D., and
M. Romer, MSW
Intruders Foundation**

ABSTRACT

A survey of UFO abductions and their associated problems in the United States adult population is reported. The after-effects of "UFO abduction" include confusion, emotional distress and strong reluctance to speak about these experiences out of fear of being labeled crazy and becoming even further isolated.

UFO abduction memories may be so unacceptable to both analyst and patient that evoking the subject matter for open discussion may be in itself be a source of acute tension. This report documents the kind of symptoms likely to be expected with abduction victims and their families and indicates the symptoms' relationship to the abduction experience. The incidence of post-abduction neurosis appears to be on the order of at least 2 percent of SICR's Patient Population. A dangerous trend is the growing number of analysts who are beginning to report daylight sightings. Additional literature and recommendations for further inquiry are available on request.

From the Musty Files of SICR

Whether it's a patient refusing to give out his unlisted number or to tell his middle name... it doesn't take much for an analyst to feel that his patients are stubbornly refusing to improve. One respected colleague had regressed to the extent that he began leaving messages in tongues on his own answering machine because no new patients had been calling him.

Another analyst felt that time had passed him by when a patient began a session with "Why does a muon act like a quark except when it's feeling like a z-buson?"

Some analysts who have become deranged from failure and frustration have been known to stuff and mount their more intractable cases.

And then there are other patients who deliver the coup de grace with the innocence of children. One spoiled twelve-year-old was discussing his weekend visit to his father's three-million-dollar beach house in the Hamptons where he spent much of his time in dune buggies. He asked the analyst, "When you were my age, did you have a dune buggy?" The analyst, who had grown up in a cold-water flat, could only think of the two-wheeler he never got for his birthday.

Transference

Among the many forces that take a heavy toll on the analyst's good humor, nothing is a insidious as "the transference." According to Freud, transference is wrongly attributing to the analyst qualities, traits, and attitudes that rightfully belong to somebody else. Transference can be inconsistent, erratic, and cruelly capricious. For every hour of the day, the analyst never knows when he will be goaded beyond endurance.

Dr. Ralph Greenson, best known as Marilyn Monroe's psychiatrist, provides us with a wonderful example of transference in action and a reason why more and more analysts are filing malpractice suits against their patients.*

"A typical example of the sudden and unexpected changes which can take place in the transference situation is the following sequence of events which occurred during a single week in the analysis of a young hysterical woman patient in her second month of treatment. She had been working well despite the fear that I would find her unrewarding and ordinary. Her feelings toward me were of awe and admiration with underlying hope that I would like her.

"Suddenly in one hour, after considerable difficulty, she admits a feeling that she is in love with me. She

---

*Ralph Greenson, *The Technique and Practice of Psychoanalysis*. Vol. 1 (New York: International University Press, 1970).

last hour when she noticed my trousers were wrinkled and my tie askew. She was convinced this meant I was not a materialist, not a greedy capitalist, but a dreamer, an idealist, even an artist. All day and all night she fantasized about me in this way; her feelings grew in intensity and she enjoyed this state of affairs. Even when we begin to analyze this reaction and trace it back to the past, her feelings persist.

"The next day she is overwhelmed with guilt. Her child has developed an earache during the night and the patient feels this was the result of her negligence; she has spent too much time daydreaming about her new love instead of caring for her child. She is convinced I must have contempt for such a frivolous woman. When I attempt to pursue the history of this reaction, she feels I am punishing her, as she well deserves.

"On the next, the third day, she feels my greeting is cold, almost a smirk, and my silence is disdain. She now feels that I am not an idealist or a dreamer careless about appearance, I am arrogant and contemptuous of my patients, who are 'poor rich neurotics.' She defends herself and her group by attacking me as one of those evil-minded psychoanalysts who lives off the rich but who despises them. She finds the odor of my cigar repulsive, even nauseating.

"The following hour she finds my attempts to analyze her hostile feelings clumsy but endearing. I am probably well intentioned and warm-hearted, only moody. I must have changed my brand of cigar and bought a more expensive one because of her criticism, and she was grateful for my consideration. She hopes I will some day become her guide and mentor because she has heard I am brilliant. When I keep silent she feels I am being 'stuffy,' conventional, and a killjoy. I probably am a grind and a hack who only loves his work. She leaves with the hurt feeling that I may be a good analyst, but she pities anyone married to me."

Where Your Therapy Dollar Goes

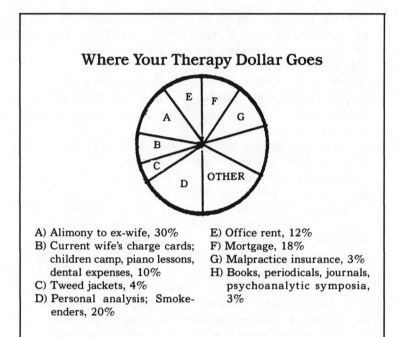

A) Alimony to ex-wife, 30%
B) Current wife's charge cards; children camp, piano lessons, dental expenses, 10%
C) Tweed jackets, 4%
D) Personal analysis; Smoke-enders, 20%

E) Office rent, 12%
F) Mortgage, 18%
G) Malpractice insurance, 3%
H) Books, periodicals, journals, psychoanalytic symposia, 3%

In the spirit of collaboration, the intelligent patient should familiarize himself with the above chart and diagram. Only by appreciating the day-to-day financial hardships and monthly budget crises his analyst faces will the patient be sincerely motivated to offer a helping hand. Patients who spontaneously offer to raise their fees, predate their checks, and pay on the first of the month are always remembered with gratitude. New York State law now permits patients to earmark their payments for the analyst's gardener, housekeeper, house and office repairs, entertainment, etc.

The worst case on record is the analyst who came to SICR because his behavior was becoming increasingly bizarre. He had sent recall notices to all of the patients he had treated prior to 1985 on the grounds that he "had forgotten to say some-

Helping the Type A Analyst

Probably the most popular course in the Neurotic Immersion Curriculum at the Learning Annex is appropriately enough called "Helping the Type A Analyst." The Type A personality is characterized by overseriousness, a compulsive concern with time, impatience, and hostility. The Type A analyst broods, feels stuck in a rut, and lies awake at night thinking of all the patients he hasn't helped.

Advanced neurotics are taught to rescue analysts from the absurdity of these obsessions and introduce them to the joys of simple being. The more courageous are taught teasing, joshing, bantering, mimicry, laughing at oneself, the incredulous expression, and mock seriousness. Helps you, helps him. The neurotic of the year, L. Flanken, cured his analyst of cigarette smoking, obesity, and hypertension in less than ten sessions.

thing." Another analyst had an air conditioner that was so loud during a session that he was totally unable to hear anything his patient said. At the end of the session, the patient turned to him and said, "That was a terrific session." The analyst slumped in his chair, looked out the window, and imagined that he was losing his grip on reality. His only consolation was Freud's cynical observation, "There is never a day so bad that tomorrow couldn't be worse."

Vainly, the analyst tries to take comfort from Freud's call to arms: "To be quite so good-natured as to let patients get away with everything and to become incapable of taking offense really ceases to be a virtue" (1903). But most often the analyst is no match for the neurotics who seem to come at him from every direction at once. Conscious, unconscious, pre-conscious, no place is safe. The analyst's thoughts reach a critical mass and he begins to lose his grip. To one patient, he says, "You've buttered your bread and now you have to lie in it." He tells another, "So what you're telling me is that when they were young, you *curdled* your children on your lap." Still another patient got a gentle pat on the cheek like in *The Godfather*.

To maintain his sanity, the analyst must resort to the absurdity of life. Patrick Mullahy, Harry Stack Sullivan's biographer, quoted to Sullivan some utterly obscure passage from one of Sullivan's papers. "I couldn't contain myself and burst out laughing. Sullivan looked at me with an expression of chagrin and asked, 'Jesus Christ, Patrick, did I write that crap?'" Even the great Sigmund Freud was only able to keep himself together with a touch of lovable nuttiness. When asked by Feiner how he managed to develop so brilliant a concept as the unconscious, he quipped, "Ah, it was just something I dreamt up on a rainy Sunday afternoon."

Chapter VII

How to Lead Your Analyst Through a Successful Course of Treatment

Know ye not that a little leaven leaveneth the whole lump. Purge out, therefore, the old leaves, that ye may be a new lump.

ST. PAUL, CORINTHIANS

What follows is a comprehensive outline of how to conduct a successful course of psychoanalytic treatment. Remember, the handwriting on the wall might be a forgery, so try to stay alert. Within each phase, I have tried to highlight the pitfalls that cause many shortsighted neurotics to fall by the wayside. The basic rule of thumb is if you want to be helped, you have to learn to give something back. Or as the Zen master said, "If he doesn't want a sweater, knit him a scarf."

The Opening Gambit

The beginning of psychoanalysis is like a chess game. There are an infinite number of openings, each of which will evoke a different response from the analyst, so choose your moves carefully. You never know how his digestion will affect *his* moves that day. Remember, there's but an inch of difference between the cushioned chamber and the padded cell, so don't you be the person who raises his blood sugar.

Now Vee May to Begin

Before you start out on a trip, you have to have a good idea of where you're going and how to get there. To begin analysis you need a good road map. One of the things you probably never realized is that Sigmund Freud deliberately invented analysts so that patients could abuse them. Freud reasoned that only when patients are invited to be rotten, contemptuous, coldly indifferent, and unappreciative toward their analysts can they be shocked into recognizing what cranks they've become.

This repetitious displacement of negative feelings Freud called *transference*. The term was originally borrowed from the Mendelsohn concept in the field of quantum physics and the third law of German thermodynamics. The concept of "Krank Energics" states that each individual has a powerful need to discharge his cranky, irritable moods and that the most likely receptacle to transfer it to is the person sitting nearest to them. In another context, Rowan and Martin addressed the same point when they said, "Grab a whole big bunch of it and throw it against the wall." Freud's hope was that over the course of time even chronic neurotics would see that their barrage of dissatisfaction rightly belonged to someone else—a person who had mistreated them in the past.

As Freud conceptualized it, all the analyst had to do was give a patient enough rope to hang himself with. Thus came the notion of "surgical detachment"—the analyst as a blank screen. In theory, an analyst would tolerate attacks on his goodness and competence until one momentous day when he would finally turn to the patient (who was beginning to feel pangs of conscience for hurting an innocent person) and say something dramatic like "You nudnick; now can we begin?"*

---

*Many analysts are unfortunate enough to have practices where the majority of their patients fail to "get it." They mix fantasy with fact and continue to blame the analyst for the whole terrible mess they're in. To reduce this misconception, SICR advises these analysts with "runaway" neurotics to hang the following sign over the couch: "Any resemblance to actual persons, living or dead, is unintentional and purely coincidental."

According to Freud, the patient's insight that he's been unrealistic, inappropriate, and churlish up to now forges a special bond of cooperation between patient and analyst. This working alliance is founded on the patient's new awareness that since he's been wrong about practically everything else in his life, perhaps the best thing to do is to be cooperative and listen to someone who knows better. By being decent and well-behaved with the analyst, the patient can finally atone for all the shabby treatment he's given others in the past.

By 1925, even Freud realized that he had left one vital element out of the mix—the human side of the analyst. He never anticipated that, given enough rope, patients might hang the analyst. (Or as he once tactfully put it, "One should never put on one's best pair of trousers.") Many analysts guiltily report a hearty dislike and feeling of prejudice toward particular patients and an impulse to do bodily harm to others. (Or as one analyst put it, "The best revenge is revenge.")* Freud called this impulse *countertransference*. In order to guard against black eyes and malpractice suits, he recommended that analysts be reanalyzed every five years to rid themselves of this bias. What he never calculated was that analysis could grow progressively longer. Now we have the revolving door phenomenon of training whereby every analyst, by the time he's through his first round of analysis, is ready to go back into it. With the institution of this practice, there's virtually no room for civilian patients.

These days, every decent analyst's caseload is so full of other analysts trying to figure out why they didn't listen to their mothers and become accountants that the ordinary lay patient has to be extremely lucky to find an analyst with any free time.

Theodor Reik, a pupil of Freud's, once explained Freud's perfectly human reaction to the erosive process of working with *meshugganas*.† "There's a big difference between theory

---

*That is what Sigmund Freud meant when he referred to "the less pleasant neurosis."

†Literally, "insane people," but most often used in a lighter vein.

Young Psychoanalyst: I have this problem. I get so
    annoyed, even angry with some patients. With
    others, I feel overprotective, even loving toward
    them.
Supervisor: Which do you consider the more serious?

and practice. A school principal had an excellent reputation for
loving kids. One day, he caught several of them playing in the
wet cement. He became very upset. He reprimanded them,
scolded them, and then he warned then that they had better
not even think of doing it again. An onlooker asked him, 'Don't
you have the reputation for being the most tolerant person who
loves to work with kids?' 'Look', the principal said, 'I love them
in the abstract. Not in the concrete.'"

The greatest myth of psychoanalysis is that it consists of a
one-sided relationship between a needy, dependent individual
and a strong, healthy, objective one. Very often, the analyst
feels like the host at a Mad Hatter's ball, but feels that no one
notices the hurts and bruises festering behind the couch. The
patient who wants his analyst to work at "a labor of love" must
learn to develop a compassion and concern for the analyst's
feelings also.

Cross-cultural support for Freud's ideas comes from the
field of anthropology. Margaret Mead reports that the only
completely happy, peaceful tribe in the world are the Papua,
residing in eastern New Guinea. When these people have a
dream in which somebody is acting lovingly toward them, they
immediately seek that person out to bestow a gift on them. If
they dream of somebody doing something bad to them, they
seek the individual out and inform him that he owes them
something.

I have recently heard of an analyst treating a patient from
New Guinea who had a bad dream and brought him a fresh
fish.

As Mead has pointed out, "More civilized people would do well to find such a balance of nature that these primitive tribesmen have discovered."

The Key to Success: Charm, Disarm, and Never Do Harm

In an experiment a number of years ago at the Mental Research Institute in Palo Alto, California, Dr. Don D. Jackson, internationally known as an expert on the psychotherapy of schizophrenia, was asked if he was willing to let himself be filmed in an initial interview with a paranoid patient who believed himself to be a clinical psychologist. Dr. Jackson agreed. "We then asked a clinical psychologist who was also doing psychotherapy with psychotics if he was willing to let himself be filmed in an initial interview with a paranoid patient who thought himself a psychiatrist. He, too, agreed. So we brought the two doctors together in a sort of supertherapy session in which both promptly went to work, treating the other for his 'delusions.' The situation could hardly have been more perfect; thanks to their peculiar state of disinformation, both behaved very appropriately and therapeutically, but the more sanely each of them acted, the crazier he appeared to the other."

Unfortunately, the experiment broke down after a few minutes when the psychologist remembered that there was indeed a psychiatrist by the name of Dr. Jackson and used the interview to discuss his own problems, gratis, with a real expert.

From the earliest stages, the analyst's task is to make his patient feel relaxed. This is difficult because he has been trained to resist the easy temptation of making small talk and so must work without conventional pleasantries. Your job is to somehow make him feel at ease while at the same time letting him believe that he is relaxing you.

A good approach is to start off by telling an amusing yet revealing incident from childhood: Your third-grade teacher asked the class for the capital of Belgium. You were called on and you proudly announced, "Waffles." Or you can tell him that in the car on the way in you were listening to Tito Puente's version of "Rorschach Test Me, Papa." All this is in keeping with the unwritten law of SICR: charm, disarm, and never do harm.

Say Id Like Id Is

Not everyone can be a Homecoming Queen, but once you start to introduce your unique brand of nuttiness, no analyst will be able to resist you. If from the very beginning you talk about the course you're taking at the New School, "Assertiveness Training in the Hot Tub," he'll know he's in good hands. One neurotic with a touch of genial nonsense started things off by saying, "Once upon a time there was a momma bear and a pappa bear and a baby bear by a previous marriage...."

With the following interchange, a depressive patient assured his analyst that a perpetually gloomy string of sessions wasn't in store for him. The patient started talking about being upset that his parents lacked normal instincts—they didn't have an "empty nest syndrome." When the analyst asked why he thought that was so, this thirty-seven-year-old patient answered, "When I told them I was moving out, they threw a block party for three hundred people."

Try to render your human foibles not only palatable but attractive and even nourishing. When you succeed in getting the analyst to be on familiar and friendly terms with you, you won't have to stand on ceremony with one another. If the start of each session can degenerate into a happy babble of irony and good-natured banter, you'll be on your way to developing what we in the trade call "an unobjectionable neurosis."

At the very first session, get your facts straight. Explain how many brothers and sisters you have, where you were brought up, and what your father did for a living.* Until they

---

*It might be helpful for you to consult SICR's monograph, "Early Memories for the Forgetful Patient."

become significant in some way, analysts have a tendency to forget these incidental matters—if one mistakenly interprets a rivalry with an older brother when the patient has only sisters, how does it matter in the long run? One approach that I found helpful for smoothing things over in these situations is to say something casual like "Oh, you mean my older brother Jane?"

Another thing to bear in mind is that the analyst is unconsciously searching for a "hook"—something that tugs at his heartstrings and helps explain it all. You can pitch in by underscoring the key events in your life. Think of a pithy anecdote, a nostalgic memory, a painful trauma. (SICR also sells a handy rear-view mirror that discreetly attaches to the patient's right elbow so he can monitor the analyst's reactions to his revelations.)

As you study your notes before each session, think of a catchy story line. The repressed experiential material of child-hood offers an inexhaustible supply of stories for you to summon up. If you don't like your own experiences, then finish this book and maybe you'll find something in it that appeals to you more. Everybody should have the right to a neurosis of their own choice. Does your story have continuity; are the characters interesting and well-developed; does it contain some pathos, a hint of sex, an uplifting message? Some tantalizing loose ends always help.

Some prize-winning neurotics have scanned the *New York Times Book Review* for interesting plots; others have found stimulating material in Blockbuster Video. If you have used all of these approaches and you still can't seem to get a rise out of your analyst, the only explanation is that he must have died several sessions ago, but since he is a classical Freudian, you didn't notice the difference.

Consider the following memorable stories from the opening sessions of highly successful neurotics, and determine which elements are likely to have attracted the analyst's attention.

• A man remembers that when he was seven, a relative asked him whether he had enjoyed his visit to the Museum of

Natural History. "No, it reminded me of a dead zoo," he said. You and your analyst can spend weeks on that one.

• A man remembers that when he was fifteen, his mother got tickets for *Hair* for his birthday for a performance during the Christmas holidays when he couldn't get off from work. Without trying to change the date of the tickets or asking the boy to talk with his boss, the mother invited one of the boy's friends to go. The patient remembers feeling nothing odd about the situation at the time.

• A man comes in and says he has led a very conventional life. His parents loved each other, there was a lot of caring and concern in the family. It was a normal household for Brooklyn in the 1950s. Of course the mother and father didn't sleep in the same room, the father didn't talk to the older brother for twenty years, the younger brother borrowed $50,000 from the patient and never paid it back, and the middle brother was married nine times—three times to the same woman. "But we all loved each other and got along, so I can't understand why you're asking me all these questions."

Dreams

Analyst love to have their patients tell them dreams because it makes them feel like real analysts. Ever since Sigmund Freud first called dreams "the royal road to the unconscious," analysts have encouraged patients to put notepads near their beds and, no matter what time of night, interrupt even their deepest sleep to write down their dreams. Thus a whole generation of patients walk around haggard, trying to fill the pad up for their analysts.

So what if you're so repressed that you have no dreams to report? Borrow one from a friend. It does little harm and makes the analyst happy. It was formerly thought that analysts thrive best on sex and aggression. In recent years, we have come to realize that it is more important for the analyst to occupy a prominent place in your dreams. If he doesn't pop up fairly frequently, try to make some room for him. He'll appreciate it.

The usual introduction analysts offer is, "We have just begun to snorkel. We are entering a new underground territory, richer by far than anything you have ever experienced in your waking life. Tell it to me in as much detail as you can." (If you can't swim, don't be afraid to tell the analyst and he'll use a different metaphor.) Try to have nice bite-sized dreams. Too long and the analyst forgets the beginning by the time he hears the end. Too short and the analyst can't make heads or tails of what you're talking about. Analysts also believe that dreams are caused by "day residues"—things that occurred the previous day that had a significant impact on you. A good patient will ask his wife right before he goes into his session, "What happened to me yesterday?"

Next, there is the matter of symbolism. Don't think your dreams are so easy for the analyst to interpret. How is he to know when a cigar is "just a cigar?" If you feel deprived because you gave up cigarettes two months ago, then obviously, in terms of the pleasure principle, if you dream of a penis it represents a cigarette. Oftentimes, however, dream symbolism is vague and impenetrable. The following chart is intended to give you the politically correct meaning of the symbols that appear in your dreams so that you can assist your analyst.

King—father (unless your father was short and inadequate, in which case Ross Perot is a good substitute).

Queen—mother (unless your mother was fat, in which case people tend to dream of their aunts).

Hat—penis (except if it's a size too small, which probably means you're suffering from castration anxiety).

Tool—generally means penis except if you're a farmer or if it's a great big shovel, in which case it's someone else's.

Shell—often means vagina. If it has sharp edges, this could mean that you think women are dangerous.

Spiders—signifies mean, cruel mothers except if you enjoyed singing "The itsy bitsy spider climbed up the water spout" in camp.

Reptile—disgust.

Airplane—you are preoccupied with how frequent flier miles "really" work.

Box—could mean vagina but in your case it has to do with something secret and hidden.

Knife—can represent protection and defense, but an underutilized theme is the unfulfilled fantasy of getting a Swiss Army Knife for your birthday.

Banana—could be a penis but also could be something you missed ever since you went on a diet. You need potassium anyway; go treat yourself.

Flowers, jewels, a well—could all be female sexual symbols or could be just what they look like. See how deep the well is in your dream—if the well is very deep, you may have a wish to enter a woman feet first.

Mountains—could be a breast. If it's Mt. Everest, your wife may be too intimidating for you to mount. Or, your mother's nipples may have been hard.

Sex

Most analysts are men. Most patients are women. Right there you have the potential for lots of trouble. Or as Freud once said, "Anatomy is destiny."

The male analyst spends long hours dealing with female patients who claim they are desperately in love with him, leading to great disappointment for both parties if these crushes don't materialize.

The analyst expects you to develop an uncontrollable desire, but he does not welcome any acting out. Analysts who have sexual relations with their patients find themselves defending malpractice suits or watching their former patients tell all on the afternoon talk shows.

In case you're really out of ideas, here's a handy, all-purpose form to use in constructing a dream: (Choose one from each list of options)

"I dreamed I was walking

	forest		banana
in a	tunnel	carrying a	pocketbook
	palace		knife

All of a sudden, I saw you walking towards me, but you changed

	Mel Gibson
into	Arnold Schwarzenegger
	Tom Cruise.

	threw up
I felt confused and then I	fell down
	ran away.

Patients who have sexual relations with their analysts can get into even worse trouble. With all the transference going on, you may find yourself committing a kind of psychic incest if the analyst reminds you of someone in your immediate family. Those transferences change so fast you could also find yourself physically involved with a relative you don't even like.

This by no means rules out a charged relationship between the analyst and patient. The ideal should be something like the first co-ed school dance: a lot of talking and titillation, but everybody stays on their own side of the room.

Analysts adore hearing about interesting new sexual positions, fantasies, and fetishes. If you've got something really hot, make a 3 P.M. appointment one day, and just when his blood sugar is dropping you can perk up that tired, jaded pro.

Analysts also enjoy talking learnedly about sex. Many give out maps and diagrams with arrows while discussing clitoral versus genital orgasms and the precise location of the "G" spot (to the left of the belly button above the hair...no, a little further down).

The first time a female patient tells the analyst she is attracted to him, he will protest that it's only a transference. "You don't really mean that. I remind you of the high school football star you were mad about." (At this point, the patient should not guffaw and tell him he reminds her more of the high school algebra teacher who had tufts of hair growing out of his ears.)

Sometimes you may notice the analyst getting a little worked up. His heavy breathing might be drowning out your words, or you may hear the telltale sound of tweed squirming in his chair. The analyst, unable to avoid staring at out-stretched limbs on the couch, may momentarily lose his professionalism and ask whether anyone has ever told you you have long legs. Immediately launch into a description of what you go through to keep them looking nice—there isn't a man alive who can maintain excitement while hearing all the details of getting a thigh-to-toe leg waxing. If he persists, repeat the part where they rip the cheesecloth off bare-handed.

There is very little problem with male patients falling in love with analysts. This is because any man secure and open-minded enough to see a female analyst probably will not be neurotic enough to need help. Also, the female analyst usually demonstrates her superior intelligence during the very first session, which intimidates most American males.

As far as attraction between analysts and patients of the same sex goes, it doesn't go too far. While the American Psychological Association has removed homosexuality from its list of illnesses, everyone knows they didn't really mean it. All analysts have gone through analysis and discovered their own latent tendencies, but they remain so scared to death of them that if a male patient so much as tells the analyst he likes his after-shave, the analyst will go into a homophobic fear fit.

Adult Children of Normal Parents

The worst thing a patient can do is be dull and boring. Learn to be versatile. Just about anything can be turned into an imaginative production as long as you stay away from normalcy. What is the analyst supposed to do with happy, carefree childhoods, close, friendly relationships with siblings, and parents who were not intrusive, rejecting, or manipulative?

Suppose a highly motivated adult child of normal parents walks in and says that he wants to explore what he has missed out on in life. All the analyst can do in cases like these is to invent a neurosis to treat.*

Analysts aren't known for creativity; if you want creativity, go to an artist. Lumpy conflict is the analyst's meat and potatoes. Grouchiness, moodiness, and even belligerence can add excitement as long as they're expressed with passion and tact. Normalcy, on the other hand, is tedious and frankly speaking, depressing. In a quiet moment, reflect on your life. Search out the drama and suspense in the commonplace. Talk in sound bites that can be conveniently repeated on the eleven o'clock news. You can also do something newsworthy like standing on top of the Stairmaster and threaten to jump. Shout out that the only person who can help you is Dr. Schwartz. "Call Dr. Schwartz and tell him to come right away, and if you need help yourself, call 1-800-SCHWARTZ, and the number in New Jersey is 1-800-394-1892."

Helping Your Analyst to Feel Valued and Understood

You can tell that you're on friendly terms with your analyst when he feels it's safe enough to ask you if you are ready to

---

*An inside joke amongst analysts that runs along similar lines goes as follows: How many analysts does it take to change a light bulb? Answer: One, but only if the light bulb wants to be changed.

take full responsibility for driving your family nuts. This is a crucial moment in treatment. The issue is: Are you ready to be flexible and give an inch? What's the big deal whether it's their fault or yours? What *is* important is that your analyst feel understood and valued. He wants you to see things his way, the right way, on a trial basis, and see whether the pants fit. Tailor yourself to the analyst's requirements.

Some analysts who wear white coats and speak in the third person sometimes get carried away with themselves. Their favorite line is, "Suppose God himself invited you into his private chambers on your last day on earth and told you what it was all about?" If you get the drift, I'm telling you what'll work. Don't settle for the common cure. Don't wait for the analyst to clear his throat, look you in the eye and ask, "Do you think you're easy to live with?" By then, it's much too late.

Okay, you're getting the idea now. You've presented a set of baffling but splendid complaints, you know enough to candidly admire the analyst, freely citing and visibly profiting from his words, and you've become a living advertisement for expanding his practice. Now you're ready for some highly classified information.

The Fundamental Rule

> It is practically impossible to speak absolute
> nonsense when one sincerely expresses what has
> crossed his mind.
>
> CARL JUNG

There comes a time in every patient's life when the analyst brings up the matter of free association. Basically, free association encourages you to relax, to have a stream of consciousness, to say whatever comes to your mind. Or as Freud put it, "Nothing you think is too small or obscure, ugly or beautiful to warrant discussion." The first thing to realize, of course, is Freud really didn't mean it. You'd better have a real good excuse for spoiling the plot of a good movie by telling the analyst the ending.

Have a little savoir faire. If you have a tendency to talk loudly and angrily while you're trying to emphasize a point, the analyst may say, "Again with the temper?" This is a code for "tone it down; the neighbors are starting to knock on the walls." If you're in the habit of wallowing in complaint-drenched monologues, have a heart! One psychiatrist got a postcard from this kind of person that read: "Having a wonderful time. Why? Why?"

If you're doing something wrong, at least enjoy it. If you say everything that comes to mind and don't give a little positive spin to things, the analyst is going to say to the person who referred you to him, "That you call a favor?"

Another thing to bear in mind is that analysts like to believe they have no specific agenda. They pride themselves on how permissive, non-judgmental, and accepting they are. "Whatever you feel, whatever hidden thoughts or impulses come to your mind, be sure to share them." It is absolutely foolhardy for you to take this too literally. Every man should catch himself in the zipper of his fly once and only once during his lifetime.

Patients have been known to recover when they've stepped on analytic land mines, but analysts have unusually long memories and have a hard time forgiving. A good example of this is the analyst Hans Sachs who made the mistake of pressing a reluctant patient, "Come, come. What do I look like?" "You look like a frog." Sachs did look like a frog. When Sachs complained to Freud that he was suffering from insomnia because of this insulting compliment, Freud advised him, "This kind of patient is the missing link between apes and human beings."

SICR's motto here, as in all things, is that "expediency is the father of all virtues." The central organizing principle to remember as you lie on the couch is to always keep an eye on the analyst in your rear-view mirror. You can never tell which way a pickle will squirt until you bite into it. Every analyst has a different kind of complex with his own sensitivities and lovable foibles. What they all have in common is that they're teetering on the edge.

The thing that most neurotics have never considered is that psychoanalysis is the art of verbally persuading a highly defensive person that white is the color it appears to be. Anything you can do to demonstrate to the analyst that you're finally becoming convinced that white is white, will calm his nerves and help preserve his marriage. Very, very slowly, he'll begin to see you as the seventh-inning stretch.

If Your Analyst Falls Asleep on You

Don't be offended, and don't embarrass your analyst by waking him up abruptly. If he's snoring, he's probably dreaming about you. Some inventive patients have used the occasion to take a little nap themselves, so that when the analyst wakes up the two of them swap dreams and engage in pillow talk. The best approach on record was a talented neurotic who sang her analyst a lullabye. Bette Midler's "Wind Beneath My Wings" seems very appropriate for such an occasion. The words read: "Did you ever know that you're my hero, you're everything I want to be..."

One analyst fell asleep and was reminded of how he felt when his mother tucked him in at night and he didn't have to be so big and smart. He woke up feeling wonderfully refreshed and optimistic and never knew why. For several weeks after that, he would wake up in the morning to be confronted by his wife demanding "Who is Joan?" "One of my patients, why?" "You keep singing her name in your sleep."

The most disarming line I ever heard was from a patient who asked her analyst, "Are you sleeping?" The analyst answered, "What makes you think so?" The patient answered, "You're breathing heavily and I know you're not having sex."

Nonverbal Communication

In order to get a good read on your analyst, you should familiarize yourself with common forms of non-verbal communication. By paying attention to the analyst's gestures, voice tone, inflections, and body posture you can gather a rich harvest of material by which to guide your actions.

- If the analyst runs his fingers through his hair or scratches his scalp, he's fast becoming puzzled, restless, and tense.* In his intensive study of anthropoid apes, Imre Herman found these same two symptoms occurred right before an ape reached out and swatted an animal he felt bothered by. Whether this finding is valid for human subjects is still under investigation.

- Even though every analyst is trained to have a noncommital expressionless face, maintaining this pose can be extremely draining. Analysts feel ashamed to be caught with an arched eyebrow, an attitude of disbelief, or an occasional grimace. Certain analysts even feel awkward if an involuntary smile breaks through.

- When the analyst repeatedly clears his throat, it is usually not repressed fellatio fantasies. He simply wants to call attention to his presence. Usually he is signaling the patient that he cannot tolerate much more, that the patient's rationalizations and denials are wearing thin. If, in addition, the analyst loosens his tie and opens the top button of his shirt, you have one more chance before he lowers the boom.

- If the analyst decides to go back to chain smoking, assume that you are personally responsible. The oral gratification that the analyst permits himself is a regressive reaction to what feels like a hopeless activity. He has no idea whatsoever what you're talking about. Since he can't control the flow of your associations, he has to satisfy himself somehow—The auto-eroticism involved in smoking is similar to masturbation. If, in addition, the analyst places his index finger alongside his nose, he is beginning to suspect that you're lying

---

*Or he could have dandruff.

to him or leaving out some important detail. If he closes a nostril with his fingers, he thinks you're a "stinker" for teasing him.

- If your analyst is in the habit of unintentionally cracking his knuckles, it suggests that he is trying to stem strong hostile feelings. His aggressive, murderous impulses are successfully channeled through the knuckle cracking, but the strong statement being made must be immediately attended to. According to Ferenczi, analysts whose feelings are getting the best of them have advanced cases of "embarrassed hands." They don't know how to occupy themselves. They can't thumb suck, nail bite, or nose pick in the treatment room, so instead they crack their knuckles and fantasize about what they would do to you if this was real life and there was no such thing as malpractice insurance.

Restoring the Analyst's Confidence

While Sigmund Freud found it relatively easy to listen without directly answering questions, today's neurotic will not tolerate frustration for very long. Time-honored techniques that patients formerly treated with respect, now result in neurotic rebellion or the termination of treatment.

Consider the following table. In column A, analysts were asked to list their typical non-directive answers to patient inquiries. In column B, we see the negative consequences of the analyst's response.

Question: Do you think you can help me?

Column A	Column B
Well, what do you think about that?	Lost 11 patients in the first year.
What do you mean by "help?"	Nine patients sullenly refused to answer. Four stormed out before the session was over.
What is your opinion?	His entire practice began paying late.

Can I give that question more thought?

Patients started talking to one another in the waiting room, asking for recommendations for new analysts.

During the 1950s and '60s, when psychoanalysis was still thought of as reserved for sophisticated New Yorkers and characters in Woody Allen movies or Jules Feiffer cartoons, a favorite joke about the non-directive approach that went the rounds was as follows:

A man tells his analyst he has an urge to commit suicide. The analyst calmly replies, "You feel excited." "Yes, damn you, of course I'm excited; I can't stand it any more." Unperturbed, the analyst continues. "You find things unbearable." "Yes," says the patient, "and if they don't get better I'm going to jump." With that, he rises and moves toward the window. The analyst replies, "You feel like jumping." "Yes!" says the patient, and he jumps. The analyst goes to the window, looks out and says, "Plop."

The low tolerance of the average neurotic for the classical approach has made many analysts increasingly confused and uncertain about what to say. Consider the following interchange:

PATIENT: Do you think you can help me?

ANALYST: Are you asking because you're worried about my ability to help you?

PATIENT: No, but I'm not sure anyone can help me.

ANALYST: What is there (about you) that makes it so difficult?

Notice now defensive the analyst gets from a perfectly reasonable question. He proceeds to pounce on the patient and attacks him for daring to make him feel incompetent.

A second example is:

PATIENT: Where do you live?

ANALYST: Are you asking because you'd like to live nearby?

PATIENT: No, that's not why I asked.

ANALYST: Am I allowed to know why you asked?
PATIENT: Well, I was just curious.
ANALYST: I am curious about why you asked.

Obviously, this patient wounded the analyst's ego. The analyst needed the patient to express a wish to live nearby. And the mean patient only seduced, taunted and teased him. The analyst then retreated, brooding over why the patient did ask.

The perceptive observer will notice that today's patient and analyst are caught in a hostile cycle that is very difficult to break out of. The intelligent neurotic is advised that all analysts want is fair play and a lighter touch. They need patients to act sensibly (like good neurotics), to rely on their own resources more, and to only ask questions that have good answers and that aren't too personal.

Group Therapy: The Couch and the Circle

Sometimes an analyst will suggest that perhaps you need a little extra help. He may advise you to join his group therapy session.

Group psychotherapy was invented by Sigmund Freud's wife, Martha, in 1909, after he told her he had too many patients and not enough hours.

Today an analyst may recommend group therapy for any of several reasons: He is usually home on Tuesday nights anyway, there is nothing good on television, and his wife keeps talking to him. He cannot bring himself to tell his most annoying patients what he really thinks of them and so has gathered a bunch of people dedicated to telling the whole truth no matter how much it hurts. He already has a place in Cape Cod and how he wants to build a ski chalet in the Berkshires and needs to improve his cash flow.

The perfect group is a microcosm of society, intended to faithfully reproduce your disturbed family of origin. In the end, you are supposed to somehow feel like you've been given a second chance and come out loving these people.

Commitment to the group is like a blood oath. Clear your calendar on Tuesdays from 7 to 10 P.M. for the next three years. If you have an uncooperative attitude about joining the group, your objections are going to be seen as neurotically destructive, self-defeating, and asocial. Besides, your analyst wouldn't have invited you unless he had already made up his mind that he needed you, so you had better go.

However, you will want to raise some objections to assure your special place in the group. Try these:

You cannot bear such a mortifying invasion of your privacy; it reminds you of being in a nudist camp. You are afraid that your revelations will be handled indiscreetly. If you tell this to the group, you will immediately create interest because most people feel protective toward paranoids.

You want exclusive possession of your analyst. Only alone with him can you live the paradisiacal fantasy of being an only child. Your jealousy is so consuming that you hated all the group members even before you met them. This kind of psychotic jealousy helps liven things up. Insist that you thought you were the analyst's only patient and enter the group by asking, "Who are all these strangers?"

Joining the group will get you only one-eighth of the time and attention from the analyst and you already feel neglected and rejected. This statement is so blatantly self-centered that the guilt-ridden analyst always will give you more attention than you really deserve.

CHAPTER VIII

The Middle Phase: Resistance and the Flight Into Health

Freud was once asked to explain the miracle of the middle phase of psychoanalysis, when all seems lost but suddenly the neurotic patient beats the odds and turns out not to be such a bad egg after all. Freud told the story of two delusional paranoids who were arguing in the back ward of a mental hospital. "I'm God." "No, I'm God." "I was God first." "I don't care, I said I'm God." Finally reason prevailed. After being at a standstill for days, one of the paranoids rose above the fray. "Okay, I'll be the Virgin Mary and you can be God." Freud's point was that if paranoids can be big-hearted, then why should a neurotic insist on being chintzy? As I pondered the meaning of all this, Woody Allen's famous line flashed before my eyes, "Cloquet hated reality but realized it was the only place to get a good steak.

By the middle phase, even the hardiest analyst is frazzled, exhausted, and depressed. He understands the traumatic effect of the transference on you. How many people can be big enough to admit that they've twisted and misinterpreted nearly every important relationship in their lives? (On the other hand, the frustrations of working anonymously make the analyst become slightly bent. At cocktail parties, when a pretty woman propositions him, he thinks she wants free advice; and he can't help reading hidden meaning between the lines of the sports column. He desperately needs his patients to bring him back to reality.)

By the middle phase, your analyst needs you to introduce a break into the routine. The most neglected feature of psychoanalytic relationships still seems to me to be the fact that it is a *relationship*; a very peculiar relationship, but a definite one. Patient and analyst need one another. You need a "toilet mommy"—someone to be a good receptacle for your pent-up feelings, but your analyst also needs you to share his own thoughts with. These include some of his innermost feelings on intimate human problems, which can grow organically only in the context of this relationship. They cannot be shared in nearly the same immediate way with a a colleague or even a husband or wife. It is also in his relationship with you that the analyst refreshes his own analysis, so if you do a good enough job, you'll save him a lot of time and money.

Tinkering With Your Unconscious Can Be Fun

In the movie *High Anxiety* the heroine is hanging precariously from a church spire while being menaced by a villain. Mel Brooks, playing her boyfriend, is paralyzed by indecision. On the one hand he wants to rescue his sweetheart. On the other hand he is terrified by heights. Suddenly, a long-forgotten childhood incident flashes before his eyes. He is sitting in a highchair and the highchair is tipping over. He feels trapped and helpless. The rest of the experience is repressed.

The hero breaks out in a sweat, glances again at his beloved. Time is ticking away. Suddenly, a curtain goes up in his mind. There are familiar faces from the past. It's his parents fighting and yelling at one another. With this revelation, our hero realizes that it is not heights he's afraid of. He's afraid of his parents. Come to think of it, it's his anger towards his parents. In a child's mind, anger is not a matter of degree; this is a death wish directed toward his parents who were always arguing. Liberated by this incredible realization, Mr. Brooks regains his courage and overcomes a lifelong fear. His anger can now be channeled toward slugging the villain.

In a nutshell, this is the essence of the middle phase of

psychoanalysis. The analyst tries to help you uncover and *work through* everything that you've managed to repress. Every aspect of your daily routine is gone over with a fine-tooth comb to conclusively demonstrate to you that your life is all messed up, your past was no better, your unconscious is worse, and that it's time to turn this insight into action. The basic idea is that if you notice what's going on, you turn out fairly healthy. As a child, though, too many things are happening all at once. Mr. Brooks, for example, was too worried about hitting the floor to think about his parents at the time. Psychoanalysis offers the luxury of one solid hour to concentrate on yourself and have it all explained to you.

The Strange Case of the Man Who Played Tennis

One unhappy patient had to be double-billed because he suffered from both penis envy and castration anxiety, and was so mixed up he wanted to fail and succeed at the same time. Many of his problems manifested themselves on the tennis court where he vehemently argued every close line call, even the ones in his favor. He insisted on using two racquets because (and this gave him away) it gave him something to do with his hands. He finally sought treatment when the net began to seem higher on his side of the court.

In the course of his analysis, the patient described a particularly painful childhood memory. Whenever he sneezed his mother would insist he had pneumonia, send him to bed for a week, and give him the most terrible tasting medicine of all time—Argorol. The cure being worse than the disease, the patient learned to stifle his sneezes and later in life made the disgusting boast that he had never owned a handkerchief. While other children were out enjoying their childhoods, this man was busy squelching his sneezes and coughs in the clothes closet.

The mother insisted she saw a fever, a rash, or a pallor whenever she looked at him. He had flat feet, a rheumatic

heart, he needed fresh air! One summer, as a show of love, she
tried to manipulate the doctor into sending him to a rehabilitation center for terminal jaundice and severe asthmatics. At last
the boy saw some hope; someone was going to talk sense to the
woman. His mother respected doctors; they would finally
convince her that the tests showed nothing, that he was
perfectly healthy.

The mother sat respectfully at the side of the desk, her
son in tow, while the doctor scanned the findings. "Madam, I
have good news for you. There is nothing at all wrong with
your son. He has the complexion of an Indian." On the way
home on the bus, the boy could see his mother having a
terrible conflict, struggling to see what life would be like if
she saw him as normal and healthy. Finally she grabbed him
by the collar and said, "See, I told you he'd call you a
paleface." Unfortunately, this woman didn't know her American history. If only she had known the difference between
Indians and palefaces, this man's entire life would have been
significantly different.

By the middle phase of analysis, the man was beginning to
get good line calls, the nets looked even on both sides, but his
racquet still looked short. Even getting an over-sized head
couldn't quite compensate because other people's heads still
looked bigger. And then there was the matter of overheads at
the net. Whenever it came time to smash the ball, there was
always the unresolved oedipus that got in the way. There was a
flinching at the final moment—a genuine fear that he could
hurt the other person—and worse, that he wanted to.

Then came that fateful day. The matter of his Aunt Sarah
cam up during a session. The patient had always remembered
his aunt as the only Jewish woman in the D.A.R. Her haughty,
superior manner always made the patient think that she
believed that her shit didn't stink. The patient suddenly had a
memory of his aunt criticizing his kind and loving mother for
how she washed her daughter's ears. Jumping to his mother's
defense, the patient had said, "My mother's a better mother

than you are." When his father came home, without bothering to find out all the facts, he attacked the boy for insulting his aunt. He moved menacingly close to the boy and asked him to apologize. He grabbed the boy by his arm. The boy reached out and seized his father by his shoulders. All at once the boy realized that he had immobilized his father. He was stronger than his own father. If he wanted to, he could push his father against the far wall. Then it occurred to the boy, if I'm stronger than my father, who's going to take care of me? With this, he relaxed his grip, became contrite, and eventually muttered an apology to his aunt.

With this wonderful association, the analyst's moment had arrived. "And now can you see why you suffered so unnecessarily all of these years? You've emasculated yourself because you loved your father so much, and your poor mother...I wish I had a mother like that." With that, the analyst could no longer contain himself. "What that woman did for you just to show she loved you. So what if there was nothing wrong with you? She needed to show her love through worry, and all those years you've made fun of her and rejected her for it. Shame on you."

This interpretation was nothing to sneeze at. The patient realized he had hidden his sneezes from his mother out of spitefulness. "Yes, yes," the analyst said. "Your mother loved your sneezes like she loved you." With this cloud lifted, the patient felt he had a new lease on life. He finally realized why lesser players played tennis better than he. It wasn't physical ability, it didn't have to do with being built small or thinking that his penis had an odd shape. His unresolved negative oedipus had blinded him from remembering to remove the racquet cover before he began hitting. With this insight, the patient became decidedly more popular at the club. His analyst was richly rewarded for his devotion by having the opportunity to treat the patient for three more years for his new, much milder obsession—an interest in experimenting with lewd, two-handed tennis grips.

Nobody in his right mind would think that a paranoid man like this patient would ever agree to such far-fetched interpretations unless he was on good terms with his analyst. The intelligent patient uses the entire middle phase of treatment to show his resilience and elasticity no matter what the analyst says or does. The trick is to respect your neurotic conflicts while realizing that in the long run it's worthwhile entertaining interpretations that make no sense at first. The "analyzable" neurotic like yourself comes to realize that what matters in the end is how much healthy ego function you can manage to exercise, not how much you feel compelled to regress. So don't mind giving up control. Life shouldn't be a power struggle. Develop the ability to work along with your analyst.

During this entire middle phase, when you're feeling better or when things get slow and you're tempted to quit, try to remember that analyst needs you (and the patients who come before and after you). With a mind like yours, he could safely confide just about anything about the human condition to you and expect empathy and support in response. It's comforting for him to hear a familiar emotion, to identify with a perfectly human predicament, to be able to stop and say to himself, "Yeah, that's how it is."

The Roar of Resistance, the Smell of the Couch

At this juncture, it might be wise to discuss resistance, which Freud defined as "anything that interferes with the course of analysis." Since that time, "resistance" has become a buzzword between analysts and patients. When the analyst says, "You're resisting," he really means, "Cut it out now." Even Kurt Eissler, the dean of American psychoanalysis, sounds flustered when it comes to this topic. "A healthy person is someone who improves with analysis." In effect, an entire generation of patients have been advised that they may not be healthy enough to even begin with analysis.

The Art of Unraveling Your Resistance

Uncovering your various resistances constitutes the warp and the woof of analysis. There are a few basic principles to keep in mind.

Resistance Problems of Different Neurotic Types

Anal Compulsive. First we should consider the anal compulsive types, who take to analysis like ducks to water (never mind that wet ducks don't fly). They describe their entire family tree in such dry, irrelevant detail that by the time they're through, all the leaves have fallen out. Where's the passion, the excitement, the really interesting trauma? If you're an anal-compulsive resister, the best approach is to quickly realize that behind your ingratiating obsequiousness, you listen to everything but refuse to get better. Share this insight ("You know, when I think about it I really don't like people") with the analyst before he gets around to discovering it and I promise you that unless he's buckled in, he'll fall out of his seat.

Narcissists. The narcissistic patient is too self-centered to really commit himself to treatment. His attitude is, "I never put on a pair of shoes until I've worn them for five years." His smugness, complacency, and complete self-satisfaction make him oblivious to the fact that he's living on the San Andreas Fault on borrowed time. These patients have the effrontery to say, "Your magazines out there have no class. I've taken the liberty of ordering a subscription to *Town & Country* and *Gentlemen's Quarterly* for you which I'll deduct from my next bill."

Continued emphasis on me, me, me, is very boring. You think you're a big shot, and you may get away with this selfish stuff with your friends, if you have any left. But your poor analyst feels completely useless and impotent. You act like you know everything already. The unanalyzed parts of the ana-

> **Silence.** Silence reminds me of the person who calls you
> up and says he has no time to talk. What do you mean
> you don't have anything to say? Your life is a mess and
> everybody hates you, and you have nothing worthwhile to
> say? Your assignment is to figure out what you don't want
> to say and then talk about it. Within the bounds of
> propriety, of sparing the analyst's feelings, talk about
> anything. The conscious "nothing" is caused by an
> unconscious "something."

lyst's personality begin to growl and act up. He is seriously
thinking of impaling you with his pen. Instead, his professionalism makes him let you off easy. He'll casually say, "You
know, low self-esteem was very big in the '80s. I believe that
you have delusions of other people's grandeur."

It was the custom amongst the Scythians to pluck out a
cynic's eye to improve his vision. Before things go too far, wake
up. Cases suffering from grandiose egos, for all their intelligence, are often very obtuse about how offensive they really
are. You could be the first case in the annals of psychoanalysis
of a narcissistic character who is actually considerate and
inquire about how things are going in the analyst's life. You
could ask, "How do I know what kind of questions to ask?" but
that just goes to show how out of it you've been all your life.
The average person seems to know, why don't you?

Hysterics. Every hysteric on record is an extremely attractive woman with long, sinewy legs and a short skirt who
drapes herself over the couch seductively but doesn't have a
clue about what she's doing. Only the hysteric seems to know
the secret of perpetual emotion.

The Problem With Acting Out

According to Freud, analysis should be carried through in an
absolute state of discipline and abstinence. All major life-
decisions should be discussed first with the analyst.

Posture. Stiffness, rigidity, assuming a fetal position, or crawling beneath the couch all indicate various degrees of character armor and defensiveness. As a matter of fact, any posture which is more or less maintained hour after hour is usually a sign of resistance. Wilhelm Reich, the "mad" psychoanalyst, suggested goosing this type of patient (but then again, he also sometimes referred to Freud as "Sigmoid," so few analysts were brave enough to follow his lead).

Resistance can take many forms. There is even one recorded case where a patient showed his lack of commitment to treatment by keeping his head elevated two inches above the pillow during the entire six years of analysis. He adamantly refused to get a chiropractor. When the analyst finally put his foot down and insisted that he realize this represented a form of resistance, the patient showed even further defiance by promptly putting the pillow over his face.

If you have nice legs, be sure not to block the analyst's view with your head. Every once in a while, turn around on the couch and engage the analyst in a little off-the-record pillow talk. A change of pace breaks up the monotony and shows the analyst that you don't live only in your own world.

If you squirm and wriggle while you're talking, the analyst will think you're keeping back a big secret. Clenched fists, arms crossed tightly across your chest, and ankles locked together are all additional forms of resistance. The analyst came into this field because he's a big noseybody. What do you want to be a tease for? One last thought. If the analyst yawns, it means he's terribly overworked. If you ever dare to yawn, you'll just about kill him.

Boring the Analyst to Death. The "model" patient is a first-class unobtrusive resister. This patient touches all the right bases but doesn't go anywhere. He has unswerving punctuality, impeccable associations, ready acceptance of all the analyst's interpretations, and typical resistances, which seem to offer excellent but tantalizing prospects of reduction. This model behavior is a very dangerous sign. For one thing, you're making the analyst feel like a failure. Another possibility is that you have a split personality and you're analyzing the wrong side.

Goethe once said, "Know thyself? If I knew myself I'd run away." In your case, that's definitely true. Your real life is the one that you don't lead and certainly aren't talking to anyone about. You have the poor analyst chasing his own tail, searching for something that doesn't exist. You're the only neurotic in the world who doesn't use repression because, sadly enough, you have nothing to hide.

What I have found in most of these cases is that the analyst can't stand the suspense much longer, so you better think of something fast. Maybe you can come up with a reverse oedipus where you're competing with your mother for your father. Or perhaps you can speculate that you're not really depressed but use that as a decoy to mask your hostility. SICR recommends dipping freely into its list of Brilliant Insights and Revelations. Please pay $1.50 royalty fee to SICR headquarters for every insight and $2.50 for each revelation.

Until any new behavior was shared, probed, dissected, analyzed, and approved of, it was labelled "acting out."

This pronouncement has left entire generations of patients in a quandary about how much they must renounce for the sake of analysis. Should they actually pass up a good promotion or forego sexual pleasure until they understand their motives better? Freud's joking reference to "sex being good but after you have it what do you have?" lent itself to much debate and misinterpretation. In many orthodox circles, it was suggested that the ideal patient could talk as much as he wanted to about sex but shouldn't have it. But other workers questioned, "If they didn't have it, what's there to talk about?" The most natural and desirable course of action is to sound out the analyst early on his specific policies about such important matters. After all, if you're going to forego sex for two, three, and even five years, you have to have some rationale handy to share with your husband or wife.

One patient recalled the day he told his analyst he had just become engaged. She looked at him silently for a moment and responded, "Yes, but has she been analyzed?" Acting out always serves the function of avoidance. Instead of discussing things within the analytic session, the patient acts upon his feelings either inside or outside the hour. This neurotic re-enactment relieves feelings and thoughts instead of analyzing them.

A homosexual man consulted the noted analyst Freda Fromm Reichman and told her that "homosexuality doesn't bother me but it does bother my mother." Fromm Reichman thought for a minute and then said, "Then your problem is with your mother." Instead of keeping this remark inside the room, the patient reported the analyst's viewpoint to his mother. That evening, the analyst answered her phone to a barrage of shrill insults and accusations. The only words she was able to make out were, "What have you done to my son?" Later that week she received a lawyer's letter telling her that she was being sued for alienation of affection. Even Sigmund Freud once complained that he knew how to deal with every type of patient except relatives.

The analyst Jules Nydes reported that an actress once offered to suck his penis for Christmas. Nydes replied, "Thank you for such a very generous offer." By thinking so fast, Nydes was able to teach this passionate creature that her unconscious was part of her; that she was not part of it. Fortunately, the next holiday wasn't until Easter.

An Overall Strategy for Taming Your Resistance

Resistance is your fault, like everything else. No matter how tolerant your analyst sounds, resistance is not something he believes is "just happening to you." Stop thinking of yourself as a passive object. Imagine you are a breast that the analyst needs to suck on. Your refusal to supply him with milk will not be looked on innocently. Analysts operate on the principle of an eye for an eye—your associations or your analytic life.

It's no excuse to stop talking because your mind is a blank or a jumble, or that you feel helpless. The analyst will keep telling you to relax, that it's not your fault, that you're not disappointing him, but don't believe it. He's lying. It's his primitive unconscious you should worry about. His head knows you're not to blame; his heart knows that if you weren't so darn perverse and unreasonable, you could get the show on the road.

The analyst tries hard not to create an authoritarian or parental atmosphere. He emphasizes that this is a relationship between two hard-working, serious adults. The only distinction is that one continuously gets fired from his jobs, doesn't have any friends, and pays $125 an hour to someone else who is infinitely smarter. The worst handicap the analyst has is that he must wait for you to discover for yourself that you're a control freak with an attitude problem. Freud said, "Analysis is like a can. It says 'to open read instructions.'" The patient said, "I've read the instructions and nothing happened." Freud said, "Insight isn't an end in itself. Insight only shows you a path. But you have to walk down it. Now stop your foolishness and get back on the couch and start working."

Clinically Proven Gambits to Disguise Your Resistance

Chances are there will be days when there is absolutely nothing worthwhile to say. But analysts abhor silences. You can fill up these awkward moments by sharing a few pithy

Resistance Analysis

The flavor of resistance analysis is best described by the following two vignettes.

ANALYST: I have had five interpretations in the last few minutes and after each one, you've negated it.

PATIENT: That can't be true.

ANALYST: That makes six.

In discussing the tyranny of the weak and how even the most brilliant analyst can easily be defeated by a willful patient, Theodor Reik told the following story. In the midst of a heated argument, a wife began beating her diminutive husband. In terror, he ran into the bedroom and crawled under the bed. "Come out!" she cried. "No!" he shouted back from under the bed. "I'll show you who's the boss in this house."

existential concerns guaranteed to create an atmosphere of ironic informality.

The analyst will be intrigued by this unexpected twist in your thinking, perhaps even mistaking you for an eccentric genius. This "halo effect" should carry over for several sessions, by which time your neurotic nature will catch up to you and bring things back to reality. But by that time, you'll have plenty to talk about.

In order to get into the right frame of mind, think of yourself as a pebble thrown into a still pond making successive rings of unsuspected magnitude.

Sure Winners
(Patient Comments)

Analyst Reaction

I am not my own opinion of myself.

Tortured neurotics are far more interesting.

I am not a helpless victim of my parents' inadequacies.	Takes responsibility. Shows capacity for growth.
I am one with the universe and I have an impact on it.	A nice touch of symbiosis.
If I have my freedom, I lack closeness. How can I be myself in relationships?	A treat for any analyst.
My neurosis feels like sounds, colors, and shapes without a home.	An artsy type—philosophical, brooding.
I have some embarrassing sex habits that are hard to share.	Good material for my next book.

Flight Into Health

No more frightening aspect of resistance exists than the notorious flight into health. In this dread disease, no matter how the analyst tries to persuade him, the patient soon feels entirely better. The analyst suggests that perhaps only the symptoms are improved, but the patient insists he feels great. The analyst goes on to suggest that his problems will only come back in another form, but the patient says he feels better than ever. Finally, in despair, the analyst says, "But you've only been in treatment for three weeks!" The intelligent patient answers, "It's been the best three weeks of my life."

Using Personal Ads to Find a New Analyst

If things are not progressing well but you don't want to hurt your analyst's feelings, you can tactfully take matters into your own hands by searching for a new analyst. Many of the top analytic journals now accept personal ads. The aspiring favorite patient can aggressively market his personality to avid analyst readers who are trying to fill their schedules with more enjoyable treatment hours.

Here are some representative ads which may help you compose your own:

SCF* tall, thin, and depressed. Good legs. On the verge of feeling better, offers vivid dreams and relates well. Looking for a well-built analyst who appreciates prompt payer with lots of good referral sources.

HIGH flying entrepreneur and overachiever suffering deflated narcissism offers a rare glimpse into the secret world of the venture capitalist to close-mouthed, politically-connected analyst who can make house or boat calls.

SMOTHERING, infantalizing and annoying 43-year-old woman, chronic martyr and sometime subtle castrator, looking for analyst who hasn't called his mother lately. Guilt provoker par excellence, ready to make commitment to long-term relationship.

WELL-BUILT, handsome, healthy neurotic available as practically normal specimen to spruce up your waiting room and cause intense sibling rivalries and feelings of inferiority among other patients. Desires perceptive analyst who can help discover the real me.

ATTRACTIVE, married neurotic, easy to please, good company, interesting history. A few shocking skeletons in closet, but mostly routine classical material. Looking for intense, short-term experience with male analyst on weekday afternoons.

YOUR GREATEST CHALLENGE. Have seen and humbled over 53 analysts of all schools, many of them quite prominent. Wouldn't you like to try your luck?

---

*Sadistic, Castrating Female.

CHAPTER IX

Helping Your Analyst Work Out Separation Anxiety: Improvement, Termination, and Beyond

Now that you have broken through the wall with you head,
what will you do in the next cell?

S. J. LEC

In the movie *Sleeper*, Woody Allen, after finding out that he had been in suspended animation for 200 years, exclaimed, "I would almost be through with my analysis by now." Certainly even you, at some time during your analysis will say to yourself, "Fun is fun, but am I getting any better?"

An objective look at your own life will not provide an easy answer to that question. You may be dismayed that you are still becoming involved in non-productive relationships with ill-mannered married men. But are any of them serial killers? There is no way of knowing how much worse off you might have been without analysis.

Don't even bother asking your analyst. Questions like this only make him feel defensive. He is sworn to the Talmudic tradition of "right back at you with the question" and will say, "Do *you* feel you're getting better? What does 'getting better' mean to you?" One patient did manage to ask her analyst, "Don't you ever do brief therapy?" The analyst responded, "All

Quick Study On How to Tell Whether Analysis is Taking Hold

Perhaps the most fundamental way of establishing whether the analysis is progressing favorably is if your analyst has begun to serve as a successful role model. Have you noticed yourself slowly beginning to identify with your analyst's ideas, values, and attitudes? In 1992, Hochspeip completed a comparative study of 10,000 women patients. What follows are the norms for women patients working with women analysts.

You wear the same earrings and use the same nail polish as the analyst.	Six months into treatment
You have the same hairdo and use the same hairdresser as your analyst.	One year into treatment
The decor of your house or apartment closely resembles the analyst's office.	1 1/2 years into treatment
Your menstrual cycles coincide.	Two years into treatment
You begin to notice that you've unconsciously named your grandchildren after the analyst.	Three years into treatment
You decide to go back to college, major in psychology, and become an analyst yourself.	Four years into treatment
Her husband calls you up for a date.	Five years into treatment

the time." The patient said, "I thought you were an analyst," to which the analyst replied, "Sometimes it takes longer."

Sigmund Freud developed the classical answer that all analysts hide behind when pressed. A man was walking in ancient Greece. He stopped and asked a bystander, "How far is it to Sparta?" The man answered, "How fast do you walk?"

The "Second Opinion"

Sometimes, despite your best efforts, things just aren't working out. You've presented all the conflicts, secrets, and significant childhood experiences you can think of, but your analyst still doesn't seem to understand you. He has made every interpretation imaginable, and not only don't you feel any better, you can't even understand what he's talking about.

The SICR way to respond to this situation is to get a second opinion...but discreetly. The very act of doing something so sneaky will leave you guilt-ridden, and your mysterious demeanor will tantalize your analyst.

The second analyst will no doubt offer an entirely different set of interpretations from the first. This knowledge is power. Pick the insights you like and use them. Think of the possibilities inherent in presenting dreams that already have been analyzed.

The first analyst will be much impressed at your sudden growth suprt; he'll develop renewed confidence in himself and his interpretations, and will be inspired by the help that you are now offering in understanding the complexities of your mind.

Always discontinue seeing the second analyst after he has served his purpose, and never reveal your little secret to your regular analyst.

Now, with the original logjam resolved, the two of you can spend many happy hours puzzling out the events in your childhood that have made you such a mischief-maker.

The Densa Post-Delusional
Improvement Test

One way of measuring your progress is by taking the Densa Post-Delusional Improvement Test. If you pass this, you are close to graduation. When it was originally introduced in 1989, this test proved to be so unerringly sensitive in tracking patient progress that SICR immediately incorporated it as part of its routine evaluation procedure. Unfortunately, with a changing patient population, there are still far too many people who imagine it might be a test for paranoia and decide they're not answering anymore no how." If you answer more than five questions as "no," you only *think* that *some* people are talking about you, which demonstrates that you are markedly improving the quality of your delusions.

1. Do you lock the bathroom door even when you're the only one home?
2. Do you shout out your own name when you're having an orgasm?
3. Are you careful about putting stamps on the envelope right side up?
4. Do you feel that the meat on your plate is staring you in the face?
5. Do you feel awkward talking on the phone when you're naked?
6. Do you believe that time is far too valuable to be wasted on punctuality?
7. Do you occasionally have the feeling that a TV broadcaster might be watching you?
8. Do you believe that when you're sleeping you're not accomplishing enough?
9. Do you believe that friends may come and go but enemies accumulate?
10. Do you believe that the incest taboo is a rule about sibling revelry?

11. Do you think that flowers are beautiful because they attract bees?
12. Do you believe you should stand aside and let the big dog eat?
13. Do you think that newsboys deliberately throw your paper in the bushes?
14. Do you have stage fright even when you're in the audience?

Termination and After

In the early 1900s when Theodor Reik was a young analyst desperately trying to eke out a living, Freud referred a wealthy German industrialist to him. The tycoon made Reik a truly remarkable proposition. If Reik would make himself exclusively available for the industrialist's use, he would be paid double his current income and be set up rent-free in a suite at luxury hotel that could be used as an office. Although he felt like hired help, Reik, newly married, accepted the offer.

What Reik remembered best was waiting for a phone call that never came. Reik recalled his services being used a total of three or four times over a six-month period. Although he received prompt payment, Reik couldn't stand the feeling of inactivity and uselessness. In his letter of resignation, his most memorable line was, "I am sorry but I am not an *ambivalence* chaser."

The moral of the story is that analysts need you to need them. The ultimate dilemma is how do you leave treatment without hurting their feelings? You and your analyst need to find common ground, a clean-cut respectful finish. To ease the pain and turmoil, we at SICR advocate "the open-ended termination." This involves a gentlemen's agreement that at the very end of treatment, if either party misses the other too much, treatment will be resumed.

The Long Goodbye

Analysts call the final phase "maturity," "autonomy," "being responsible for yourself," or "taking charge of your life."

Despite the winding down phase of treatment, your analyst will tend to make interpretations that indicate a softer, kindlier look at your life. "Your father was not necessarily rejecting, he may have been self-absorbed. He wasn't indifferent, he was preoccupied." When you think of how your father's father treated him, you realize how lucky you are.

At the end of treatment, you come to realize that things weren't so unfair after all—and even if they were, none of it matters so much and the rest of your life is up to you. Your analyst is in good spirits. He tells you the story of a man who goes to the priest and tells him all his sins and asks for forgiveness. The priest thinks for a minute and says, "It's too late." The analyst pokes you in the ribs and says, "You prove them wrong."

Your parting gift to your analyst should be to help him work thrugh his own separation conflicts. Sigmund Freud advised that it is correct techique in the termination phase for the analyst to make self-disclosures that wouldn't have been appropriate at an earlier phase of treatment.

Despite this sanction, your analyst will be reluctant to share his life with you even at this late date unless you bother to ask. With your help and encouragement, he will be able to let his hair down, sift through the ashes of his life, and provide some insight as to why the loss of you on his couch is a deep and meaningful hurt.

As the two of you discuss the rush of unconscious meanings and memories evoked by the impending separation, a special bond is forged. By this time, any guilty remnants of the hurt, suffering, and disappointment that you once inflicted on your parents are long since gone.

In these, the twilight hours of your analysis, you must wean the analyst gently. Keep going for an extra year or three.

Gradually shift your focus to the outside world by bringing up topics such as the Academy Award nominations.

Just when you have turned into the sort of nice, friendly person your analyst might actually like to know better, you are not going to be talking to him anymore. This is patently unfair and potentially traumatic to him. Do what you can to rectify the situation. Form an alumni association of former patients who will sponsor an annual testimonial dinner for the analyst. Name a constellation in his honor. Refer him a couple of patients to take your place. Send cards and flowers on Freud's birthday. Remember him in your prayers, and before you leave promise to have nice dreams about him for the rest of your life.

The Patient Hall of Fame

In analytic circles, allusions to certain patients are made in hushed tones, with a reverence reserved for only a select few. Some patients, like "Wolf Man," Dora, and Little Hans, are classic studies because their pathology was so unique. Others are immortalized in the SICR Hall of Fame in Vienna because of the joy and satisfaction they brought to individual analysts.

Ted M. — Amassed a perfect attendance record of 1,257 consecutive sessions over a seven-year span despite an appendectomy and two gall bladder surgeries.

Robin M. — Made timely payments for her entire course of treatment (48 months).

Jordan R. — Filled his analyst's entire practice within two years after he entered treatment by referring eleven co-workers, twelve relatives, three friends of the family, and fourteen people he met on the golf course.

Alison M. — A virtuoso patient whose personality was so powerful that her analyst was cured of all the allergies he had suffered since childhood.

Chelsey M. — Was married to her analyst for two years before she realized he was no longer her analyst.

Peter C. — Saved his analyst's daughter from death by strangulation when he said, "Don't worry, it's covered by the insurance," after she backed into his brand-new Mercedes in the driveway outside the office.

Cameron R. — Won the award for the most inventive excuses for missing a session for the years 1990-91 and 1991-92. On one occasion, Mrs. R. reported being kidnapped by the Mafia and being let off on the East Side where she couldn't catch a cab because it was rush hour. Another time, she said she was abducted by UFO creatures who didn't believe her when she told them that she was going to be charged for the session she missed.

Postscript to the Emma Case

In "Depression, Despair, and Dyspepsia" Sigmund Freud gives us a rare glimpse into the personal *agita* involved in being an analyst. In a mysterious footnote to this work, Freud comments, "I have never been quite the same since I started treating Emma von R. She is more trouble than two Wolf Men and one Little Hans." For years, scholars have debated the true identity of this maddening woman who could drive even the great Sigmund Freud to confess tha "she is the only patient I deliberately gave the wrong interpretations to."

In 1984, with the release by The Library of Congress of Freud's private papers and personal diary, we were finally able to piece together the only case which Freud acknowledged to be a therapeutic failure. Theodore Reik, an associate of the master, remembers Freud saying, "I have always believed that when it comes to a sense of justice, compassion, and consideration, I have been a dedicated analyst. Emma von R., however, has taught me that it is not a bad thing once in while to go against one's principles and habits. This impossible person has introduced me to all hidden sadism and primitive hates that I never knew I possessed. Many's the time I had to restrain myself from leaping across the couch and telling her what I really thought."

The Strange Case of Emma von R.

Emma von Rosensweig first consulted Sigmund Freud in 1909 at the age of 33. She was a stern, unappealing woman of stocky appearance with a reputation for being the wealthiest woman in Europe, heiress to a vast lox fortune. Her presenting symptoms were insomnia, fatigue, and a terrible red rash that covered her entire body during moments of stress. During the first months of treatment, Frau von R. responded favorably to Dr. Freud, during which time her symptoms started to lift.

One fateful day, Freud opened Pandora's box. "Perhaps you red rash is your way of identifying with and competing with your father's first love, his precious Nova Scotia. The jealousy and anger that you feel inflames your passion and eroticizes your skin. The only realistic hope of cure lies in finding a fulfilling relationship with a man. Therefore, I am prescribing regular doses of a normal penis."

The Red Herring Theory

Emma von R. was repelled by such a lewd suggestion. The very idea that her prim Victorian unconscious could contain such animalistic ideas was too much for her and she fainted. When she revived, Freud tried a different tack by approaching her sympathetically in her natural tongue. "You seem to be floundering," at which point Emma began heaving and sighing hysterically. Wondering what dark forces he had unleashed, but still not grasping what she was getting so excited about, Freud mumbled under his breath, "Smelts fishy to me."

Emma von R.'s faith in Freud was shattered forever by these, the very first Freudian slips. She soon dropped out of treatment and spent the rest of her life villifying Freud's great reputation by bad-mouthing him up and down the Carpathian valley (saying things like "That man has a dirty unconscious."). Periodically, she sent him poisonous reminders of his great insensitivity to the pathos of her circumstances.

Finally, in 1913, Freud had his last contact with Emma von R. On August 9 of that year, Freud wrote, "... you are terribly mistaken if you suspect that I harbor a personal prejudice or dislike toward you. The fact is that I have come to the wholly objective scientific opinion that even your unconscious is not very likable.

"Because of my relationship with you, I have redefined the superficial meaning of sadomasochism, have developed a tic over my right eye, and now smoke six cigars a day. For all these reasons and more, please refer yourself to Dr. Carl Jung in Zurich. Knowing him, he will probably enjoy working with somebody such as yourself..."

The Birth of SICR

When the author was nominated for the Nobel Prize in 1988 for the concept of the Super-Id and Wa-Wa Theory of Development in Psychoanalysis, the scientific community was shocked that such a simple notion could explain so much.

As you all know by now, the id consists of all the primitive drives and needs in man that press for expression. Sigmund Freud suggested that the superego is the source of conscience and guilt that keeps this baser side in check. The psychoanalyst is a sort of gate keeper. He must have a more highly developed superego than most because he must renounce so many normal human impulses. I went Freud one better and suggested that because the psychoanalyst spends his entire career personally delaying gratification and professionally denying every selfish pleasure, he must possess a "super-id."

What I meant by this is that so much frustrated emotions must be damned up in the psychoanalyst, there must be so much deprivation, that it is only natural that he would be subject to unbearable stresses and strains. I spent twenty years investigating the powerful "wa-wa" instinct in analysts—an overwhelming impulse to cry out despite it all. This uncivilized, shameful urge remained unresolved in the psyches of many analysts.

Then one day in the fall of 1984, a remarkable event occurred that changed the entire course of human history. I had accidentally parked in a stranger's driveway. When I returned to my car hours later, the householder had left a brief note. It read, "My dear sir, you have parked in my driveway so I was unable to get my car out the entire day. Please be more careful the next time. Also, you left your headlights on so I took the liberty of turning them off." At first, my thoughts became quite paranoid. What damage had he done to my car? After examining my car carefully inside and out, I realized that when he had all the reason in the world to be rageful, this unknown stranger was actually kind and generous. I was thunderstruck. I was the recipient of an act of generosity that was beyond my power to grasp; it humbled me and made me ponder how to repay such remarkable behavior.

Altruism and Forgiveness

Suddenly, it all came to me at once—the cure for neurosis and the birth of SICR. Analysts cannot express what they really need; they are sworn not to show it. If you, the patient, can demonstrate altruism, compassion and, unconditional love despite your neurotic condition, not only will you make him happy, but in one fell swoop you will have found a way to redeem yourself.

As if to confirm this theory, I had a wonderful dream that night that one of Superman's arch villains challenged the man of steel to lift a huge statue of a cat that was in the entranceway to a temple in Bangkok. Whereas ordinarily Superman would have had no trouble at all, this time around he almost developed a hernia. Superman was lifting the cat with ease, but he was also lifting the entire continent of Asia which happened to be attached to the cat. Instantaneously it came to me that this dream dramatically represented the terrible burden of being a psychoanalyst. Every analyst as a child is recruited to bear the responsibility for his entire family, to make up for what is lacking in his parents' life, to be the good one, the understanding one, the family bellweather.

The unconscious rebellion against such a unnatural role was shown by Sigmund Freud when at age seven he deliberately unrinated in his parents' bedroom. "Piss on you, mein Herr," was Freud's heroic response to his oppressive parents for having to sacrifice a real life in the service of being the family hero. In *"Only a Prisoner of Childhood"* published in 1983, undoubtedly my greatest work, I remember saying that being a psychoanalyst is an impossible profession but trying our best seems to make a difference.

Analysts Take It Hard

Every analyst, beginning with Freud, has his bad moments. Once, in accepting an honor from the B'nai Brith in Salzberg, Freud quipped, "Thank you for the beautiful award; I really don't deserve it. But then I have migraines and stomach cramps and I don't deserve them either."

To cite just two examples from SICR's case files of analysts who fell apart when patients left without saying goodbye: We have the tortured delusional poems of Ludwig L.

Unconditional Love

I am a nice boy,
More than just nice,
Two million times more,
The word is Adorable.

Next we cite an example of the bitter, cynical edge of a depressed analyst, Morton von K., who wrote the following poem to himself:

Who cares?
Who could?
Who should?
Who needs it?

Dr. von K. abandoned a promising career because of his doubts about the profession and went on to write the popular best-seller *Nobody Loves Me*.

A Sampling of Freud's Letters to His Favorite Patients

"See what happens? I live gloomily and in darkness until my fifty minutes with you. After your departure, I have eyes to see again. Even Martha doesn't look so bad" (Freud, letter 101).

"I am in a rather gloomy state and all I can say is that I look forward to our sessions as to a slaking of hunger and thirst. I shall bring with me nothing but a pair of open ears and shall be all agape, waiting to hear your latest bit of mischief" (Freud, letter 48).

"You can have no idea how much you last visit raised my spirits. I'm still living on it...I need you as my audience" (Freud, letter 103).

"I felt wonderful after our last session last week. Your terrific insight perked up my spirits to such an extent that I raised all my fees. Before you, I had been without anyone who could actually teach me anything" (Freud, letter 6).

February 30, 1991

To: SICR Members

From: SICR Analyst Incapacitation Committee
         S. Raymond, Ph.D., and J. Fiszman, Ph.D.,
         chairmen

Re: NOTIFICATION AND ASSISTANCE TO
         PATIENTS IN THE EVENT OF INCAPACITY
         OR DEATH

Most of us do not like to contemplate our own mortality. Analysts, particularly, prefer to labor under the fiction that they are immortal. But this comforting thought should not deter us from making plans for the continuation of the care of patients when something happens to us.

In an attempt to implement a plan in the event of one's incapacitation or death, we are suggesting the use of the following checklist. It should be kept in a special file and a spouse and/or colleagues should be informed of its existence. If and when the analyst decides to resume his practice after his death, the patients will be contacted and advised that they can have their old hours back if they call immediately.

Checklist of Procedures in the Event of Incapacity or Death

1. Designate two or three colleagues to notify patients and assist spouse. These colleagues should be previously consulted regarding their availability to serve in this capacity and to consult with patients regarding interim therapy, resumption of treatment, and/or referral.

Name of Colleague   *Phone Number*

_____   _____

_____   _____

_____   _____

2. Until patients can be contacted by these colleagues:

   a. Telephone Answering Machine:
      Leave as is; collect all messages.

   b. Telephone Answering Service:
      If caller asks about previously scheduled appointments, advise, "The doctor's schedule has been temporarily cancelled. Someone from beyond will be contacting you shortly."

   c. Office Door:
      Place note on door indicating, " The doctor's schedule has been cancelled. Telephone the doctor's office."

   d. Compile a list of names, addresses, home, and office numbers of current patients and attach to checklist. Keep this list up-to-date.

   e. Attendance of patients at funeral or memorial services. Patients should be informed of such services since, for the most part, this confirms the reality of the loss of their analyst and facilitates grieving. If you plan to resume your practice after your death, you may not wish your patients to attend the services. You should indicate this so that patients can be so advised.

The Successful SICR Graduates' Poem

"Autobiography in Five Short Chapters"
by Portia Nelson

I

I walk, down the street.
There is a deep hole in the sidewalk.
I fall in
I am lost ... I am helpless
It isn't my fault.
It takes forever to find a way out.

II

I walk down the same street.
There is a deep hole in the sidewalk.
I pretend I don't see it.
I fall in again.
I can't believe I am in the same place.
but, it isn't my fault.
It still takes a long time to get out.

III

I walk down the same street.
There is a deep hole in the sidewalk.
I see it is there.
I still fall in ... it's a habit.
my eyes are open.
I know where I am.
It is my fault.
I get out immediately.

IV

I walk down the same street.
There is a deep hole in the sidewalk.
I walk around it.

V

I walk down another street.

We shall not cease from exploration
And the end of all our exploring
Will be to arrive where we started
And know the place for the first time.
                    —T. S. Eliot, *Four Quartets*